Sport and Physical Recreation

2nd Edition

Ian T. Elvin

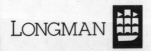

Longman Group UK Limited
Westgate House, The High, Harlow, Essex CM20 1YR
Telephone (0279) 442601
Fax (0279) 444501

First published 1990
Second edition 1993

A catalogue record for this book is available from the
British Library.

ISBN 0-582-22811-5

Printed in Malaysia by TCP

Contents

Acknowledgements

The preparation of this book has been a response to years of involvement and experience in sport and recreation. In trying to present material which satisfies the needs of ILAM I am also conscious of the requirement to identify with the varied perceptions of the reader. This book may be read by students, practicing managers, or sports administrators and therefore it must seek to inform and explore issues which are of consequence to the profession of leisure management. The text does not assume prior knowledge of certain organisations that are deeply and directly involved in sport and recreation. My involvement in sport, and the experience and satisfaction of working with undergraduate students, trainee managers and leisure managers has resulted in this work. For their role in this I thank them.

The inclusion of specific material used to illustrate contrasting sports organisations was made possible through the encouragement, support and ideas that I was offered by them.

One of the major difficulties in preparing a relevant and topical text for a constantly changing sport and recreation environment is actually keeping up to date and presenting only those issues of keenest interest. There has been material left out of this text due to natural editorial constraints. Every effort has been made to be up to date but it is recognised that circumstances, particularly those that are political, can and do change in fairly unpredictable ways. The pace of change in the United Kingdom, as far as sport and recreation is concerned, suggests that we must regularly monitor specific opportunities and constraints. There has been every effort made to present issues which are topical and typical and as such their relevance may be just as pertinent in a few years time.

Sport and Physical Recreation examines the organisations most involved with the provision and management of opportunities and facilities. This includes central government, local government, quasi-independent bodies and a variety of organisations from the private sector. The approach to each one is through an exploration of their role, an examination of management related issues and comment on possible improvements or developments to out sporting culture. Case studies and practical examples drawn from sport and recreation illustrate the fascinating variety and complexity of issues that affect managers. In seeking to develop a client centred approach this text aims to be relevant, topical and informative.

It is impossible to commit time and effort to maintaining a love of sport, a desire to contribute to the management and promotion of sports and prepare a text like this, without the support of some very special people. Janet, Richard and Catherine are very special people and I thank them.

Ian Elvin

Preface

Recent years have seen the expansion of leisure services throughout Britain, whether they are provided by institutions in the public, commercial or voluntary sectors. Such leisure facilities and services are now recognised as of critical significance in the changing social and economic structure of contemporary Britain: this has been acknowledged by the Government through the recent establishment of a Ministry for National Heritage led by a Minister of Cabinet rank. The effectiveness of such provision, however, lies in the hands of leisure officers and managers and it is clear that there is a need to ensure the highest level of professional support for leisure services.

The Institute of Leisure and Amenity Management (ILAM) is in the forefront of developing and promoting schemes of professional education and training leading to qualifications and a higher level of competence of personnel in the Leisure Industry. The nineteen-eighties and the early nineties saw the ILAM Certificate and Diploma with hundreds of examination applicants. The establishment of Industrial Lead Bodies and the identification of competencies in the form of National Vocation Qualifications (NVQ's) and Scottish Vocational Qualifications (SVQ's) at at least four levels are other recent advances. Further consideration will be given to levels 5 and 6 at a later date. These professional qualifications are designed to ensure that Leisure Managers and their supporting personnel have a sound base of education and training to enable the competent day to day operation of leisure facilities and opportunities. Similarly there is a concern to ensure a thorough knowledge and understanding of the disciplines and skills appropriate to managers in the leisure business.

The aim of this series is not only to provide texts which will cover constituent elements of the earlier ILAM syllabus but it will provide a base of knowledge and examples that will allow leisure professionals to update and improve their practice and managerial skills whilst ensuring the competent functioning of their junior staff. In that sense the series will not only be relevant to ILAM courses, Higher National Diploma and Degree qualifications but will also act as a reference source for trainee professionals and personnel entrusted with the development of the NVQ and SVQ framework.

This text aims to provide the leisure manager/student with an insight into the main issues surrounding the management of sport and physical recreation. The book will serve to enhance and develop an appreciation of the knowledge and skills required of the manager within this distinctive sector of the 'Leisure Industry'. The book starts with an essential review of recent trends in outdoor recreation and sport and includes an exploration of the influence of a range of socio-economic and demographic factors on these patterns of behaviour. A detailed examination is then undertaken of the role of different organisations who have a critical part to play in providing for (and influencing provision for) sport and outdoor recreation – national and local government, the Sports Council and other national agencies, the governing bodies of sport and the commercial and voluntary sector. The text is liberally supported by case study examples which illustrate the critique provided of sport and outdoor recreation activities and facilities. The book concludes with an identification of the issues that have to be faced in the future organisation and management of these major areas of leisure activity.

Brian S. Duffield

Series Editor

Introduction

For the majority of people in the UK the opportunity to participate in some form of sport or physical recreation is not a real problem. Whether interest lies in the outdoor environment or in built facilities, our expectation has grown towards convenient, well organised, efficiently managed opportunities.

Many of the general public, the paying customers, will however not understand who manages, or even who owns, a facility. To them what really matters is the friendliness of staff, the quality of service and an acceptable price.

Whereas the pleasure-seeking public may overlook who is actually providing the opportunity, and who is delivering quality service, the managers are clearly in a different position. Essentially this text is geared to managers, actual or aspiring, who will be accountable for their own performance, to the staff who work with them, and to the success of their organisation in achieving declared objectives.

Since there are so many organisations involved with sport and recreation, too many to cover each one in depth, it becomes important to identify foci which provide appropriate features of successful practice. In addition, it is necessary to be aware of key issues which influence, or effect, the day to day operation of an organisation. Although a number of organisations will be featured and key issues addressed, ultimately it is the manager who will need to consider those questions which most affect the operation of his or her organisation. A systematic approach to undertaking an internal evaluation of the organisation will need to follow certain rules or benchmarks of good practice.

Britain benefits from a wide range of organisations involved with sport and recreation. These include:

1 National and local government.
2 Quangos (quasi autonomous national government (or non-government) organisations).
3 National and regional associations.
4 Governing bodies of sport.
5 Local clubs and societies.

6   Public companies which may be national or multinational.
7   Private clubs.
8   Industrial (employer) sport provision.
9   Media (press, radio and television).
10 Entrepreneurs (promoters, event managers and agents).

Even people heavily committed, either to one sport, or to one organisation, can easily become confused when considering the complexity of the organisation of British sport and recreation. As the pace of change and the competition for business increases, so the need is established for a more sophisticated manager who has a clear understanding of the markets, of the opportunities that might be available and of the critical areas of competition. No meaningful attempt at solving disparate problems can be presented in a few pages, nor can a model strategy for all British sport and recreation be achieved here.

The prime goals of this text are to:

1   Present a clear overall impression of how sport and recreation is organised in Britain.
2   Provide a number of examples of organisations which seem to illustrate the British way of managing opportunity in sport and recreation.
3   Indicate critical areas of concern both for customers (sports people and recreationists) and for those who service their needs (the managers).
4   Suggest positive ways in which organisations may become more flexible, adaptable and responsive to market forces and customer expectations.
5   Establish an impression of how sport and recreation organisations can prepare longer term strategies.

This text provides a contribution to the study of British sport and recreation. In particular it is designed to focus on the needs of those working, or seeking to work, in the sport and recreation sector. Examination success for students and managers will be a by-product of reading and interacting with the material presented. What really matters is how the reader can better understand the organisations and the processes, and perhaps become a little more adept at recognising the needs of the public and the parent organisation.

Undoubtedly the character of any association, concern, company or corporation, and its ownership, will determine which particular markets it will serve and what activities and services are to be offered to the public. Each and every organisation must in itself become fit to achieve targets and respond to change.

In order that the reader recognises and accepts the basis on which this text is prepared a brief review of content and progression might be useful.

Chapter 1 focuses on the frequent debate surrounding definitions, particularly of sport and recreation. Managers need to understand behaviour and trends in participation and the historical background to these trends if they are to appreciate fully the role of sport and recreation in our society.

Any text which examines the nature of organisations involved in sport is almost bound to start with a consideration of central government. Chapter 2 identifies the character of British government, paying particular attention to England and Wales. Although occasional reference is made to Scotland and Northern Ireland the main area of study is limited to England and Wales. The important feature in this chapter, which is relevant to all who study the subject, is the relationship of sport to central government. Arising from this will be specific issues of interest to managers such as the changing role, or influence, of central government over sport and recreation.

The nature of delegated authority from London considers quasi-organisations and their relationship to government. Compulsory Competitive Tendering (CCT) and the contracting of services will continue to play a major role in redefining the responsibilities of quasi-government bodies and local authorities in their relationship to higher authority.

Chapter 3 examines the impact of local government on sport and recreation. This includes a profile of local government services and issues like CCT, contract management, quality systems, sport equity and their impact on the provision of sport and recreation.

The Sports Council, being the most significant quasi-government body responsible for sport, is considered, in Chapter 4, in its role as an enabling organisation. The re-organisation of the Sports Council, with the addition of a UK Sports Commission and recent strategy documents, provide obvious points of reference since the attitude of government, and the response of sports agencies, are clearly influenced by them. Regional councils for sport and recreation have had a fairly wide remit and are included in this chapter due to an obvious identification with the Sports Council.

The Central Council for Physical Recreation (CCPR) conducts its affairs largely on behalf of the voluntary sector representing over 200 sports or activities. In a similar vein the National Coaching Foundation (NCF) provides services for coaches in all sports and the Institute of Leisure and Amenity Management (ILAM), the Sports Aid Foundation (SAF), the British Sports Association for the Disabled (BSAD), and the National Playing Fields Association (NPFA) each represent one facet of British sport and recreation. Chapter 5 seeks to define a role for this selection of organisations and to explain their relevance to managers.

Chapter 6 identifies a number of British governing bodies involved in indoor sports as illustrations or case studies in the private sector. Some management issues are common, particularly those with resource implications. Facility needs and the development of each sport is considered in turn. A discussion of issues of interest to outdoor sports governing bodies contrasts with a case study on tennis which focuses on a feasibility study of an indoor tennis centre and its subsequent development.

A case study based on one sports club forms the basis for Chapter 7.

Although the material directly relates to one rugby club many of the organisations previously discussed are considered in relation to a specific problem. The possible loss of playing fields is in itself a major issue.

Continuing the organisational context Chapter 8 considers the commercial sector. Appropriate case material from one company is used to illustrate primary management issues in the profit seeking sector. A sports organisation servicing a major employer provides the focus for a wider debate on management effectiveness in achieving agreed objectives.

To appreciate an operational context it is necessary to consider the availability of facilities for sport and recreation, both in indoor and outdoor provision. Chapters 9 and 10 achieve this through an account of the British model of provision, and include reference to additional relevant organisations. A case study of one local authority complex presents an examination of how one facility was conceived, planned, developed and subsequently managed.

Direct first-hand involvement in sport remains a recommended means of understanding organisations at a local level. These few chapters present a wider view of sport and recreation at a national level, hoping that the reader can appreciate more fully the fascinating complexity of British sports organisations and issues.

Practical implications for sport and recreation managers will be determined by prevailing local circumstances, and as such this text does not propose to cover all issues. Certainly those factors which are likely to affect a wide section of managers, in the public and private sectors, are considered, but it is for individuals to determine relative significance. In providing a basis for managers, and aspiring managers, to understand the organisational context, questions arise regarding the future of British sport and recreation. These are either implicit or explicit in this text but they form the rationale for what the future may bring. The trend of continued change seems to emphasise a move towards a more business orientated approach where the need for effective and efficient managers will become increasingly important.

The future for British sport must also be seen in the context of a country seeking to emerge from an economic recession, one where there is continuing pressure on public spending both within local authorities and the quasi-organisations. Indeed the governing bodies of sport and their constituent parts must also seek an increased measure of self sufficiency in their work. The generation of additional financial support for sports organisations is likely to become the responsibility of specific organisations established for that purpose and not simply central government. Certainly future funding of sport through a national lottery, a charitable foundation, and the encouragement of partnerships with sponsors is likely to provide an important source of additional money required by a variety of sports organisations. These range from governing bodies and clubs to local authorities and community-based groups.

1 Defining sport and recreation

The terms, **Sport** and **Recreation** are so often used interchangeably that we need to ask, why bother with definitions? If a function of an organisation is to promote a certain activity then it is the image of that activity that is paramount, and not necessarily the label attached to it. It is afterall the quality of experience that the manager is trying to provide. A few parameters should assist an appreciation of the two areas:

Sport includes:
1 Elements of competition.
2 Physical activity.
3 Aspects of organisation.
4 The influence of outcome on quality of experience.

Recreation differs in certain ways:
1 The focus is on activity *per se*.
2 Satisfaction is gained primarily from the quality of the experience.

Many physical activities seem to be able to lend themselves to both sets of parameters. Horseriding, golf, running, gymnastics and swimming are essentially individual pursuits. Since the infrastructure required to turn them into sports is not complicated, we can clearly see that what we are dealing with is individual perception.

Certain tensions experienced by those participating in team sports or group activity, including the desire to win, can, in part, replace the desire for satisfaction in the quality of experience. It is unlikely we would see a game of rugby, football, hockey or netball, for example, being played in an organised fashion where the final score, or winning, didn't actually matter to those involved.

Just as team activities are more easily defined there is also a noticeable difference in perception between elite performers and 'the average participant'. An accomplished sportsperson usually finds satisfaction in winning, or in a good measured personal performance. That athlete may, however, become more relaxed and less ambitious when playing an alternative sport in which he or she does not excel.

Fundamentally the need is simply to appreciate customer perception, recognise the necessity for providing opportunity, and cultivate customer awareness of the scope of experience that an activity can offer. Ultimately it is for the individual to decide upon participation, and the selection of personal goals, both qualitative and quantitative, or both.

Since the opportunity to participate in sport or recreation requires facilities, the central task of organisations, and associated individuals, is to provide a service which focuses on people and which satisfies need.

Organisations and trends in participation

Organisations operating within sport and recreation must understand the markets they serve and those trends that may influence future behaviour if they are to compete for both leisure time and the leisure pound. Not only should the provider consider the appropriate level of supply, and the perception of customers, he or she must also recognise the character of our society and those demographic relationships which could shape or determine areas of growth, or decline, in participation.

In a society which is made up of the broadly defined groups indicating wealth and employment on the one hand, and poverty and unemployment on the other, there is a need for accurate information on existing and potential markets. Every organisation in both the public and private sectors should seek to achieve targets and satisfy objectives which are based on such information. National and regional trends, population forecasts, economic prospects and an appreciation of social forces each contribute to investment decisions and feasibility studies. The development of sport and recreation requires policies which are regularly reviewed. All organisations require regular advice on the development of their corporate strategies and a review of policies and practice if they are to succeed.

It is possible to trace the involvement of government, both centrally and locally, with the development of both an organisational infrastructure and purpose built facilities. The UK did experience a period of rapid expansion of facilities, especially with indoor sport and recreation centres, during the mid 1970s. This expansion was followed by the doubling of participation in indoor sports between 1973 and 1977. Patterns and trends in participation must therefore acknowledge the significant contribution that new facilities or opportunities can provide.

Historical background and participation

The number and character of sports organisations, facilities, and patterns of participation have origins far earlier than the 1960s. Although further information is included in subsequent sections, a brief and recent history, from 1960, will serve to illustrate growth patterns.

Relative prosperity, evident in the UK during the 1960s, was represented particularly by:

1 Increasing car ownership.
2 Shorter working week.
3 Longer holidays.
4 The promotion of leisure pursuits.

These factors encouraged wider participation in sport and recreation. In 1974 local authority re-organisation gave further stimulus to the development of facilities. Comprehensive departments were created to manage the new facilities and provide specialist advice to elected members.

When looking at the range of activities and facilities from the point of view of the consumer, it is important to examine the nature and extent of influences on participation. These factors determine what a person might do and which organisation he or she could approach. Personal and social constraints are largely beyond the control of the manager, but there is a need to be aware of such personal features as age, stage in life cycle, sex, and marital status. Such an appreciation becomes more complex when one includes characteristics such as attitudes, skills, fitness, and cultural background.

It is important to appreciate that there is a complex relationship between personal and social factors, notably where it affects:

• income
• car ownership
• employment characteristics (including holidays, hours worked)
• time available for recreation
• the influences of friends
• education
• social and cultural forces.

The manager is concerned with acquiring a sensitive awareness of these issues. Providing opportunities for individuals in the community requires knowledgeable organisations.

Participation in sport and recreation continued to grow through the 1970s, although certain groups seemed disinclined to take part. The 1980s were characterised by the emergence of strategic approaches, including those from the Sports Council, governing bodies of sport and recreation, and local authorities each seeking to promote participation to disadvantaged or under-represented people.

Sport in the Community, Into the 90s, A Strategy for Sport 1988-1993, published by the Sports Council, concluded that inadequate resources and insufficient progress led to some previous Sports Council's targets not being met.[1] Other comments suggested that:

1 Although more women are taking part in indoor sport the number of women participating in outdoor sport has fallen.

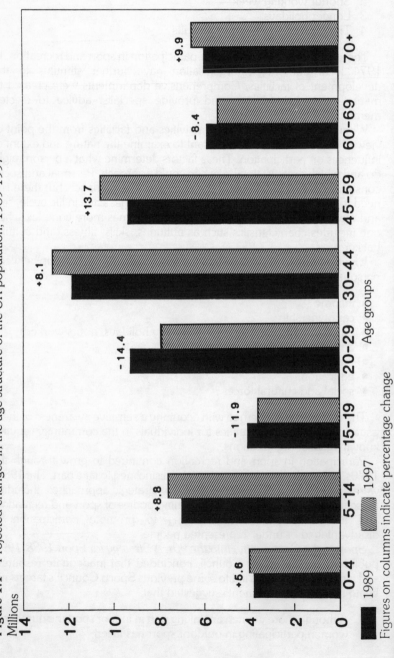

Figure 1.1 Projected changes in the age structure of the UK population; 1989-1997

Millions

Figures on columns indicate percentage change

2 Participation by men has increased, both indoors and outdoors.
3 A disappointing number of young people have come into sport. This has in part been compensated by the increase in interest of those who are middle-aged or older.
4 Activities associated with 'a healthy life style' have enjoyed an increase in participation. These include jogging, swimming and cycling.
5 When dealing with performance and excellence the Sports Council expresses disappointment with the lack of coordination between organisations.
6 The National Coaching Foundation has been a real success and prospects for the continued development of coaching services, and participation, look reasonably strong.

The 1980s provided a period of radical readjustment both to the economic and social make-up of the UK. Politics, never far from the scene, were responsible for some redefinition of goals. Indeed, it may be felt that government and Sports Council's encouragement for individual sports bodies to prepare their own objective strategic documents could eventually lead to increased participation.

Demographic factors

Of perennial interest to organisations in sport and recreation will be the population trends and how they may affect participation. Figure 1.1 provides a clear indication of the estimated changes in the UK population between 1989 and 1997. It is predicted that there will be an increase in the number of children under the age of 15 years and that there will be significant decreases in the 15-19 years and the 20-29 years age groups. The major growth predictions for the 0-14 years will start to decrease by the year 2003, falling to pre-1994 levels by the year 2009. There will be a change from decline to increase in the number of 15-19 year olds from the middle of the 1990s. An important effect on the future levels of sports participation will be created by the decline in the traditionally more active young adult population. There will be a drop in numbers of the 20-29 years age group, an increase in 30-44 year olds and a decrease in the retired population until the end of the century. The effect of these changes highlights the need for greater awareness of the changing demographic patterns and what they will mean for any given population and a specific sport. With fewer people in the traditionally more active younger population, a potentially larger mature age group, an important ethnic minority population and the requirement to have a regard for the sporting needs of people with physical, sensory and mental disability, sport providers are obliged to be constantly aware of their market and its needs.

Figure 1.2 profiles a decade, 1981-1991, of falling population in a number of English regions together with predicted changes for the period 1990-2001. Of course examining data for the whole country, or even just for one region, is insufficient. Organisations also need to be aware of:

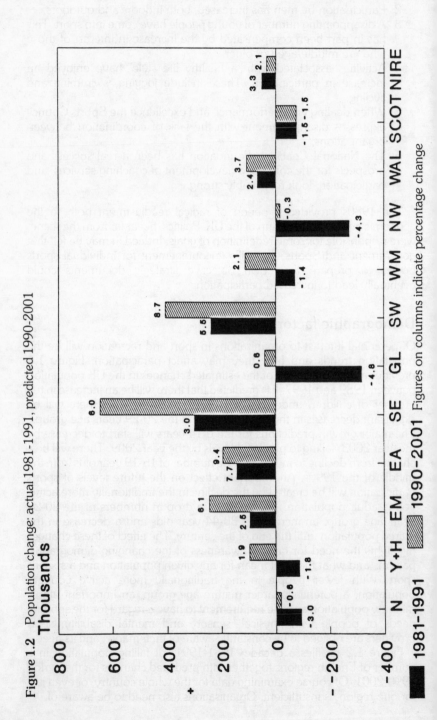

Figure 1.2   Population change: actual 1981-1991, predicted 1990-2001

1 How the population is changing nationally.
2 Any significant regional or local variances from the national trends.
3 Anticipated differences between the changing populations of rural and urban areas.
4 What effect projected national population changes might have in coaching, administrating and participating in sport or recreation.

Previous data has indicated general trends in participation, but it is the demographic downturn in active populations that is likely to hit the traditional areas of recruitment the hardest. The post-school tendency to opt out of sport has been well documented, certainly since the Wolfenden report in 1960.[2] More recent research suggests that young people do remain interested in a range of physical activities, that they do not usually drop out of sport when leaving school, indeed they are committed to trying new activities both during and following school years. Although boys are more likely to participate in sport than girls, girls are just as interested.[3,4] It is important to recognise that the reduced population of school age children, including the 15-19 age group, having already been introduced to sport, may continue with a sport active life style after the age of 25. Outdoor sports that attract these age groups must consider their recruitment strategy over the next eight to ten years. The sports of football, athletics, tennis, cricket, rugby, all traditional British sports, and amongst the most popular, could be the hardest hit. Two factors could ameliorate this situation:

1 Participation trends are improving in the 'older' age groups.
2 Any enhanced drive to attract young people could sustain current numbers. It might also provide the skills and awareness necessary for later initiatives when the population decline has slowed down. Whilst it may be difficult for all sports to maintain previous levels of involvement those that have active youth development schemes could enjoy the benefits of higher participation.

Access considerations have rarely been focused as they now are, by age, and especially on those who are middle aged or older. To look a little further, say over the next ten years, the age group 30-59 will assume even greater significance for managers, particularly as some sports attempt to make amends for any fall off in younger participants. Two thirds of British sports take place outdoors and well over 12 million people claim to participate in them.

Participation in outdoor sport and recreation

The General Household Survey (GHS) used a revised methodology in 1987 to improve accuracy concerning participation rates enabling a comparison, for the first time, in 1990.[5] Walking, two miles or more, remains the single most popular outdoor activity both for men and women. In the most popular quarter of 1990, over 20 million adults

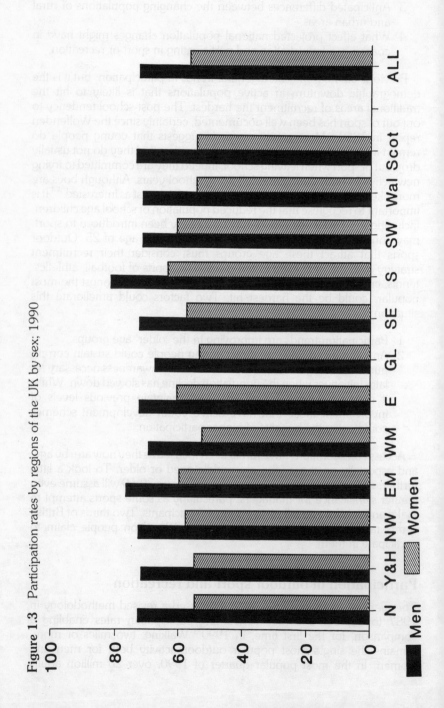

Figure 1.3 Participation rates by regions of the UK by sex; 1990

reported walks of over two miles. Indeed it far outweighs the popularity of swimming, which is the next widely available sport or recreation. One of the more interesting changes from 1987 to 1990 has also been the marked increase in recreational cycling. In fact the interest in road running races and marathons seems to be levelling off as cycling and swimming continue to increase.

Just as team games appear to be experiencing something of a downturn so there has been a positive increase in activities which can be undertaken without partners and with the focus on health and fitness. Hockey is an exception with a 200 per cent increase in adult participation; a factor largely explained by the success of the British team in the 1988 Olympics and the growth in numbers of artificial pitches.

The development of interest in health and fitness largely explains the growth of participation in sport across the different age categories; one that is growing fastest with the middle-aged and the elderly. Women's participation in outdoor sport has tended to remain static or even decline.

There are differences (shown in Figure 1.3) in participation between the regions of England just as there are distinctions between England, Scotland and Wales. Some of the differences can be explained by the rural or urban dimension rather than by a regional or national perspective; however outdoor participation was clearly lower in Scotland and Wales, even when walking was included. Overall the GHS of 1990 does provide evidence of increased sports participation of about two million people between 1987 and 1990. Preference or choice might well come into the decision making process. Although it might be reasonable to suppose that an overview of participation in any sport is the most relevant factor, it still seems appropriate to ask governing bodies and local authorities what they are doing to encourage women into outdoor sport. National development plans prepared by governing bodies are one thing, locally based initiatives are another, sometimes costly option.

An appreciation of markets and trends, both for the participant and non-participant, should enable organisations to recognise and respond to new priorities. A proactive stance is required; one where organisations examine where they would like to go, and where they have come from.

Assumptions regarding patterns of participation may need to change. Certainly no one can ignore the enormous wealth of opportunity that exists with 8.5 million people aged 65 plus (97 per cent of whom are not working) now living in Great Britain.

A strategy for sport

What emerges from the information available on participation is that:

1 The nature and variety of sports and recreation available may continue to broaden both in scope and number.
2 Health related programmes will continue to develop and they appear set for a period of sustained growth.
3 Clearly differentiated policies will be required by organisations in

order to match demographic trends, patterns of mass participation, and the development of excellence with the opportunities available.

Role of sport and recreation in society

Having briefly discussed definitions for sport and recreation, sports participation and the requirement for information and awareness, there is a need to expand the discussion somewhat. So far our attention has been focused on those who are 16 plus years of age. Children have therefore been excluded from the discussion. Just as adults participate in sport and recreation for a variety of reasons, so too do children. It has been clear that people, young and old, participate partly for friendship or companionship. Social groups operating through sport are well recognised.

Children at play also enjoy and benefit from social experiences. Practical involvement in play is important for children and the opportunity for constructive play also entails freedom of expression, spontaneity and satisfaction. These value statements may be related or overlap but we should recognise them as the basis for the need to play.

Since participation in play, sport and recreation has a significance for individuals and/or groups the social context for this should also be understood. What role do sport and recreation play in our lives? Are they simply a health and social facilitator? Does participation simply provide some escape from the rest of our lives? Organisations should try to understand the motivations of individuals and the decisions which, when made, might promote participation. The need for an acceptable image has been discussed. Satisfaction based on the quality of experience is difficult to measure but it is very important to the individual. If organisations wish to promote an effective development strategy, it is imperative that they try to understand the expectations of the individual.

Organisations and issues

In a free and democratic society one would expect to see a tremendous variety of organisations and associations in sport and recreation; in this the UK is no exception. Sport in the United Kingdom has evolved like a patchwork quilt, namely :

1 A lot of hard work has gone into making it the way it is.
2 Much of what you see has been made out of whatever materials were available, and over a period of time.
3 The product is attractive and largely successful, although there appears to be a considerable diversity of colour and shape.
4 It is difficult to suggest fundamental change without taking the whole thing to pieces and starting again.

Organisations in sport and recreation face increasing economic pressures. Managers, in coming to terms with these pressures, need to be aware of any underlying financial and political constraints. Performance in achieving organisational targets will be open to scrutiny, particularly if they involve external resourcing. Some specific examples of these pressures will illustrate this diversity. Grant aid for governing bodies, particularly from the Sports Council, is increasingly targeted on specific objectives and accountability is keenly sought if continued assistance is to be available. Maintaining the quality and quantity of facilities both in urban and rural settings have been under pressure for some time. The need for voluntary organisations to be self-financing, and the limits imposed on local authority spending, have effectively brought sport and recreation into an economic environment requiring sound management practice. Although the balance of financial constraints may vary between town and country, managers are still encouraged to satisfy demand and locally determined objectives.

Professionalism, competencies, and the ability to deliver customer care have become increasingly important. Not long after some sports have gone open, and while others continue to discuss the difficulties surrounding professional and amateur sportspeople, the spotlight seems to be falling on the sports managers and administrators themselves. Delivering the necessary management skills and producing a well conceived product have become essential, it seems. Marketing skills, including the generation of sponsorship money, will continue to be a high priority for organisations who are not guaranteed financial viability.

Issues such as the impact of the National Non-Domestic Rate on the voluntary sector, compulsory competitive tendering and contract management, or the privatisation of water have also been of importance to the executives of national governing bodies, the Central Council for Physical Recreation and the Sports Council.

The introduction of the National Non-Domestic Rate in April 1990 affected sports and recreation, particularly in the voluntary sector, in a number of ways. Clubs are now defined as business organisations even though they may not operate purely for profit. Every club was reassessed for a charge which replaced the previous rates and came into force on 1 April 1990. The ability to pay any possible increase was potentially offset by a system of relief from the National Non-Domestic Rate based on a transitional period. Prior to April 1990 councils were empowered by the General Rate Act of 1967 to grant mandatory relief of 50 per cent to registered charities and up to 100 per cent discretionary relief to organisations, not operating for a profit, which were wholly or mainly used for purposes of recreation. The amount of discretionary rate relief to non-profit-making sports clubs varied across the country, with many local authorities offering no relief at all. Some local authorities regarded the operation of a bar as a reason for not awarding discretionary relief. The Local Government Act of 1988 (Section 47) provides for a discretionary rate relief to non-profit-making sports clubs in England and Wales of up to 100 per cent.[6]

The regions of Scotland can also offer 100 per cent discretionary rate relief to non-profit-making sports clubs, whilst in Northern Ireland there is a statutory 65 per cent reduction for non-profit-making sports clubs.

After 1 April 1990 registered charities in England and Wales received 80 per cent mandatory rate relief. Local authorities were given the discretionary power to grant relief in excess of 80 per cent with 75 per cent of the discretionary sum coming from the non domestic rate pool.

One important difference existed following April 1990, namely that the Department of Environment, in their guidance notes, stated that the existence of a bar should not be a reason for not giving discretionary relief. Local authorities are now required to consider the purpose of an organisation when examining the case for discretionary rate relief.

With central government now prepared to share the discretionary rate relief in the proportion 3:1 there is every encouragement to sports clubs to apply. Local authorities will, of course, be required to pay 25 per cent of the rate relief granted.

Many urban-based outdoor sports rely on local authority facilities, games fields in particular, but activities based in rural environments also rely on rights of access, formal agreements or the goodwill of private land owners. In both cases, however, much of the activity is actually organised through the members of a club or society. Those groups therefore look for leadership and support from their governing bodies. As many sports grow in popularity, and as increased encouragement is fashioned to bring people into active life styles, so the ability to deliver the right product, and to satisfy customers, becomes increasingly important. All this has a wider spin-off, not just for public authorities and governing bodies but for the future of British sport in general.

Local authorities will be particularly sensitive to the needs of clubs and organisations that use public facilities. The management of these facilities post competitive tendering, and the availability of suitable provision for the voluntary sector, are issues that should concern local authorities and governing bodies alike.

Forward planning is vital, or do we, as a nation, continue to improve the quality of the patchwork quilt, through occasional repair or piecemeal replacement? Or should there be greater coordination of effort? Local authorities, governing bodies, local clubs or groups will always play an integral role in the delivery of opportunity or services, but might this not be aided by a national development plan for sport, one that actually enjoyed central government political backing and the necessary financial support? Perhaps some of the opportunities and constraints that will emerge might encourage the debate.

Sport has become, and will remain for the foreseeable future, a major industry. With approximately 20 per cent of total consumer spending committed to leisure and nearly £6.6 billion of this bound for sports, there are clearly opportunities for continued investment.[7] Increasingly the public and private sectors are working in partnership to promote leisure initiatives. At a time when local authorities are experiencing financial constraints, a flexible approach can have clear advantages. Furthermore, any apparent health and growth of the economy suggests that leisure projects, if not always sport and recreation, may continue to offer a sound financial return.

The intrinsic values of participation, health and fitness and a positive life style continue to be important. Developments over recent years in the public and private sectors indicate that a major contribution is being made by sport to both local and national economies. Central government earns a significant income from sport-related taxation. The government and the economy also benefit from equipment purchases, the income derived from participation and the spin-offs into associated service industries. The image portrayed by our 'traditional national sports' is rather narrow and limiting. However, as society continues to evolve, identities can be influenced, even changed! Is there equal opportunity for particular disadvantaged groups? Local authorities have, in many areas, encouraged certain activities, rather than others, simply in the pursuit of welfare or social benefits. Central and local government have a distinct responsibility for health and welfare. Participation in sport and recreation therefore deserves to be fully recognised and supported with adequate resources.

Summary of key points

1 There are a wide variety of organisations involved with sport and recreation covering both public and private sectors.
2 Those involved with either mass participation and/or excellence are in the business of identifying and satisfying the needs and aspirations of members and customers.
3 It is the perception of the individual regarding the character and quality of the sports or recreation activity that is central to the evaluation of organisational success.
4 Understanding demographic profiles provides a necessary insight into changing markets, real or potential.
5 Central and local government have played a critical role in the development of opportunity to participate in sport or recreation.
6 Participation in sport has developed over twenty years of increasing prosperity and consumer choice.
7 Certain disadvantaged (or under represented groups) continue to exhibit lower levels of participation.
8 Organisations should avoid generalisations and assumptions about the character and needs of the users.
9 Central government should play a major role in encouraging participation in sport and recreation.

References

1 The Sports Council 1988 *Sport in the Community, Into the 90s.*
2 The Wolfenden Committee on Sport 1960 *Sport and the Community.* HMSO, London.
3 The Sports Council 1988 *Sport in the Community, Into the 90s.* P 9.
4 The Sports Council 1992 *Sport in the Nineties – New Horizons.* a draft for consultation.

5 Office of Population Censuses and Surveys 1990 Series GHS No.21.
6 Local Government Act 1988. HMSO, London.
7 Henley Centre for Sport Forecasting 1991 *Leisure Futures*.

Further reading

Peter McIntosh and Valerie Charlton 1985 *Study 26: The Impact of Sport for All Policy 1966 – 1984*.
The Sports Council 1982 *Sport in the Community: The Next Ten Years*.
Chris Gratton and Peter Taylor 1992 *Economics of Leisure Services Management*. Longman/ILAM Series.

2 Central government and sport and physical recreation

The government of the United Kingdom is expressed through a parliamentary democracy, with a constitutional monarch as Head of State. It is the character of central government, and the political party in control, that exerts both power and influence over the legislative process. Parliament makes the laws and the Prime Minister, the Cabinet and other Ministers, plus the civil servants in government departments form the executive.

Although the political party that commands a majority in the House of Commons forms the government, it is the independent judiciary that determines the law and interprets statutes.

All organisations at a national or local level must follow the law of the land which is supreme. Sports clubs and local authorities, for example, must recognise this fact when determining laws or rules.

Although sport has been at the margins of political debate in the United Kingdom, it is the nature and structure of central government that clearly explain current ideologies and management, and therefore exert a measure of control over sports.

The ability of sports administrators, professional bodies and representative groups to organise effective pressure on Parliament and the executive is clearly important.

Issues such as drugs in sport, safety or facility provision at football clubs have attracted political interest in central government and legislative controls can be used.

Sport and the Department of National Heritage

The Sports Council is generally recognised as the executive arm of government concerning the implementation of policies for sport and recreation, but for 30 years the department responsible for sport in central government has enjoyed the services of the Sport and Recreation Division (SARD). Policy formulation and development has rested with SARD, but over the years it has been difficult for central government to coordinate all matters concerning sport because a measure of responsibility was allocated to various departments in central government.

Given that until recently there was no single coordinating department for sport and recreation, the Sport and Recreation Division has moved from time to time to a number of departments. In the three years 1989 to 1992 responsibility for sport was first with the Department of Environment then, for a brief period, with the Department for Education and Science before moving to the new and current home in the Department of National Heritage.

The decision in 1992 to form a new department, and accord the Secretary of State for National Heritage a place on the cabinet has achieved a number of milestones. It provides the opportunity for sport to be considered at the highest level of decision making, it presents the Minister with the opportunity to argue for adequate resources for his department's responsibilities, it ensures that key areas of responsibility, previously spread across a number of departments, are brought together in one department and it secures a focal point for all matters concerning sport and physical recreation. Nevertheless, sport and recreation is just one area of responsibility in a department which also includes arts, tourism and heritage.

Not only did SARD transfer to the Department of National Heritage, a number of civil servants working in areas which had become a responsibility of the new integrated department were also transferred.

Other departments involved in sport and recreation

At the same time as the formation of the Department of National Heritage, the Department of Environment and the Department for Education retained certain responsibilities which have an influence on sport and recreation. The Department of Environment is still charged with the overall responsibility for planning and the Department for Education has the remit for the National Curriculum and Physical Education. Any debate concerning the law and safety at football grounds will involve the Home Office, but the responsibility for the National Lottery is with the Department of National Heritage.

The Department of the Environment is responsible in England and Wales for a wide range of functions, including public expenditure and local government, regional matters, planning, development, control, regulation of pollution, water and sewerage, countryside affairs and so on. Some of these duties still affect sport and recreation, including advice and guidance on planning criteria. For example circular PPG17: *Sport and Recreation*, published in 1991, is just one paper which will have an important bearing on the future protection of land for sport. This planning and policy guideline is an influential document which establishes sport and recreation as an important element of civilised life and proposes that a value should be attached to protecting open spaces with a recreational value.

The Department for Education, responsible for the promotion of education in England and Wales, has specific charge for school and post-school education. In 1988 the Education Reform Act[1] gave rise to a debate on the role of physical education in school, focusing on the contribution made to each child's development and the prescribed school time table allocation.[1] The legislation which directs school programmes, and has a bearing on sport and recreation, clearly affects other public and private organisations. The introduction of a National Curriculum, including compulsory physical education for school children until 16 years of age, is an important element of the department's responsibilities. Coming at a time of financial constraint in schools the introduction of the National Curriculum in physical education, from 1992, presents particular problems regarding the ability of schools to deliver all required courses. Concern continues to be expressed over the availability of resources to fund swimming, outdoor and adventurous activities. There is a recognition that a lack of appropriate skills in the teaching of dance, outdoor and adventurous activities, combined with the general shortage of specialist skills in primary schools, may influence the quality of work and assessment. With the introduction of the National Curriculum and the constraints on resourcing sport and recreation for school children the distinction between physical education and sport and recreation is becoming more pronounced. Leisure departments and national governing bodies, with their development function, are having to assume a greater responsibility for extra curricular activities and for sports competitions. If there is to be a clear separation of sport and recreation from the rest of physical education in schools the responsibility for the welfare of children will need serious consideration. At the same time extensive opportunities are likely to open up to children for involvement in new sports and in a wide variety of activity.

The Home Office deals with internal affairs in England and Wales that are not within the remit of other departments. Criminal law and public safety are areas of accountability although the Department of National Heritage is responsible for the implementation of sport specific reports such as Lord Justice Taylor's Report[2] on safety at football grounds.

Central government has devolved elements of administration to Scotland, Wales and Northern Ireland.

Scotland, with a cabinet post for the Secretary of State for Scotland, has its own legal system and some administrative autonomy. The **Scottish Education Department** has a particular interest in sport not just through the education system but also through the operation and financing of the Scottish Sports Council.

The Secretary of State for Wales, a Cabinet Minister, has, for example, full responsibility for planning, tourism, national parks and the Sports Council for Wales.

The Northern Ireland Office is the responsibility of the Secretary of State for Northern Ireland. As in England there is the Department of Education and the Department of the Environment with a specific interest in matters relating to sport and recreation.

Sports issues and central government

Changes in British society over the last 20 years have been significant. The role of government in that time has also changed markedly. When considering the impact of social, economic and cultural changes it becomes necessary to examine the relationship between central government and sport.

The House of Lords Select Committee debated sport and recreation in 1974 having published two reports a year previously.[3] It was primarily interested in the coordination of policies for informal outdoor recreation and in the need for provision of opportunity to participate. This was followed, in 1975, by a White Paper (Cmnd 6200), *Sport and Recreation*, which also considered 'principles of policy' and 'a programme of action'.[4] Coming just after the establishment of the Sports Council, these debates represent the arrival of sport and recreation onto a political platform. Although they are now matters of history, the contents of the Select Committee Report and the White Paper provide interesting illustrations of political perceptions of sport. In the 1975 White Paper *Sport and Recreation*, an expression of intent is clearly made:

It is not for the government to seek to control or direct the diverse activities of people's leisure time. Nor do the government wish to adopt a paternalistic attitude to the many different providers of recreation in this country. (paragraph 14)

Events in recent years, however, do not quite conform to the sentiments of the White Paper. There has been a clear and firm encouragement towards sports adopting systematic management and control. Organisations in government and those relying, directly or indirectly, on financial support have all been required to identify clearly defined objectives and appropriate measures of performance. Efficiency and effectiveness have become central to the operation of many sports executive committees either voluntary or paid.

Certainly life has changed from the 1960s and 1970s when central government was generally satisfied by the intentions of local government and governing bodies of sport. Building facilities and providing sport and recreation at subsidised prices were then seen as a satisfactory way of catering for the needs of the country. It was appropriate to build facilities where it was felt they were needed. Efficiency could be measured by relating activity to existing structures, rather than by examining performance targets and a rationale for the organisation's existence. In the 1980s organisations in sport and recreation began to examine quantitative measures of performance and economic measures of efficiency.

Indeed, the National Audit Office was established by the government as an independent body, seeking to determine value for money and giving advice on changes in central government's attitudes towards spending state funds.

Sport, central government and delegation of roles

Central government through the 1980s and early 1990s has not sought to overtly manage sport and recreation Although departments may have a keen influence on policies, powers have largely been delegated to public, quasi-public and private organisations.

Central government places a permissive power only on local authorities to provide sport and recreation facilities. The only obligations are for library services, youth and adult education in recreation, social and physical training and the provision of allotments according to demonstrated need.

With sport receiving low political status, and the allocation of permissive not mandatory powers, central government exerts its influence in a number of ways.

Laws are created which direct change. The privatisation of state owned industries, compulsory competitive tendering, regulations concerning planning and the National Non Domestic Rate (or the Uniform Business Rate) as it affects sports clubs are examples of legislation determining new directions. Government also influences via circulars, procedures, advisers and regional offices. Quasi-independent organisations, such as the Sports Council and the Countryside Commission, offer an explicit interest in sport and recreation.

Central government, in offering no direct encouragement to local authorities to develop policies for sport and recreation, has constrained local policy makers. With no contextual framework local authorities have tended to develop services in a rather inconsistent fashion. Although efficiency and effectiveness have become watchwords for any organisation hoping for, or relying on, financial aid, there has still to be a clear and positive encouragement to develop or support sport and recreation programmes. The delivery of an appropriate service has yet to become a priority.

Quango bodies (quasi Autonomous national government organisations)

The fragmentation of administrative structures at central government and the lack of a national policy for sport and recreation have long represented an argument for establishing an integrated department. A focal point for leisure, incorporating sport and recreation, it would not only lend political weight to what is now a significant service industry, it might also encourage local authorities to confirm leisure policies as an important element of local service. Clearly the Department of National Heritage will play an important role here although there does not appear to have been any substantial shift of government policies regarding sport and recreation. The government's attitude from the mid 1960s has been to devolve responsibility to the various quasi-independent organisations established to service certain needs. Consequently the development of ideologies and policies has been through those quasi-government bodies. Grant aid to the Sports Council, for example, has always been insignificant in relative terms, which confirms the low political status afforded to sport and recreation. Nevertheless over the last two decades the Sports Council has assumed a pivotal role for government in the delivery of 'sports policy'. Established in 1965 as an advisory body and then in 1972, by Royal Charter, as an executive organisation with independent status, the Sports Council has in fact mirrored the will of central government. Grant aid to the Sports Council for most of its work comes from the Department of National Heritage. The Royal Charter made it clear that the relationship between the Council and central government was not just based on goodwill. Indeed, the Minister for Sport's Review on Sports, published in 1991, highlighted the need for reform of the present structure of the Sports Council' ... and that ... 'the government proposes to replace the present GB Sports Council with a UK Sports Commission and a Sports Council for England.' Such a proposal required the surrender of the Royal Charter and the agreement to distribute responsibilities anew. The Review primarily concerned England and Wales but it did examine issues that have an impact on Northern Ireland and Scotland.

Although a subsequent section of this text examines the role of the Sports Council in some detail, focusing on its organisation, relationship with government and key issues affecting British sport, it is worth identifying the most salient consequences of the Review since some of them go beyond the role of quasi-independent organisations.

Sport and active recreation

The Minister for Sport in 1991, Robert Atkins, undertook a review of sports policy and published a statement which largely focused on England and Wales, with some matters of interest to the UK. The review itself is not particularly significant for the detail or information it contained.

Although some important outcomes were proposed the review also provides a moment when sport and recreation gained further political attention. The review reminded British sport that the government did not see itself as a key player, but that it looked for others to support and encourage through their own policies and programmes. With regard to central government the review reaffirmed previous policies which define an arm's length approach. The proposed function of a new UK Sports Commission, replacing the GB Sports Council, and the establishment of an English Sports Council, with each organisation working in specific and defined areas, is intended to provide a more coherent structure and the re-organisation targeted for completion in 1993. Further details on this issue are contained in Chapter 4 on the Sports Council. The Minister sought to promote the development of business sponsorship for sport by promising what has become Sportsmatch. The review effectively confirms government attitudes towards a number of items; it welcomed the establishment of the British Sports Forum as providing an important opportunity for member organisations to represent the UK voluntary sector and it recognised the contribution of government in establishing the Foundation for Sport and the Arts.

It is still apparent that what we have in Britain is meaningful state intervention through particular schemes and state-derived apparatus. The quasi-independent organisations, together with appropriate resources, provide the means by which the political will may be exercised. State intervention has been significant. The introduction of the **Foundation for Sport and the Arts** and moneys made available through **Sportsmatch** provide an indication that a shift in responsibility may be taking place. One that distances the state apparatus from decisions concerning grant aid. With 40 million a year available from the Foundation and 3 million of government money devolved in England to the Institute of Sports Sponsorship (in Scotland and Wales the responsibility lies with the respective sports councils) significant grant aid decisions for sport have moved one step from government. The test of how far this political shift might continue could be determined by the system of managing the grant aid allocation for sport from the national lottery.

Whatever the conclusion regarding the mechanism of allocating money from a national lottery quasi-independent organisations appear to provide a depoliticised instrument of state. Central government can be neither directly accountable for its failings nor the object of scrutiny by the sports lobby. Critical appraisal is therefore deviated from central government towards the necessary quasi-independent body.

Organisations such as the Sports Council therefore act as a buffer or conciliator between pressure groups like national governing bodies and the state. **The Central Council for Physical Recreation** represents the views of national governing bodies to the Sports Council who in turn are responsible for representing those views to government. Since the Department of National Heritage grant aids the Sports Council, which in turn considers need for financial support from various organisations, the relationships are fundamental.

It is the ability to pay for sport and recreation that underpins the approach to provision both nationally and locally. Indeed 'Sport for All' policies have influenced both the Sports Council and the local authorities for the best part of 20 years. Publicly organised subsidised sport and recreation is based on the need to satisfy disadvantaged target groups and to provide equity in provision. There are strong arguments for suggesting that this ambition has not been realised because policies and strategies have not matched priorities with targeted funding. This issue is one being considered in the latest review of the Sports Council's strategy.

Health, education and social welfare have long been instruments of persuasion in favour of promoting a positive and active life style. Collective consumption is a principle under close scrutiny. If state funds are designed to make up for the deficiencies of a commercial sector, or to overcome gaps in provision, then some quantification of objectives and the extent to which those objectives are met is clearly important. The 'Sport for All' philosophy masked the truth concerning participation trends. Not only have socially and economically advantaged individuals and groups been benefiting from subsidised services, but there is insufficient evidence of local authorities researching or gathering data to establish the extent to which they have successfully reached target groups. Local authorities have a responsibility to the community they serve which goes beyond a recognition of market forces.

The voluntary sector seen through thousands of sports clubs and societies is increasingly recognising that 'survival is dependent on its own efforts'. Sports clubs and societies exist because they satisfy the needs of members and do so only within the resources that they raise. Increased competition for members, a diversification of life styles, and demographic trends need to act as a stimulus to the voluntary sector. Central government does have an important role here through the encouragement of club activity. The efforts made in this direction can be achieved through Sports Council grants, local authority assistance and relief from National Non-Domestic Rates (Uniform Business Rate). The voluntary sector has been described as the backbone of British sport and for that reason is worthy of government assistance in one form or another.

Government intervention in the management of sport has redefined the role of the state. All agencies, including the centrally appointed quasi-independent bodies, must recognise the 'new' managerialist approach and accept that from time to time there will be government intervention. In addition there has been only limited indication that the promotion of sport will enjoy any additional commitment from the government. Grant aid to the Sports Council will at best largely remain in line with inflationary trends. The development of relevant services, the maximisation of resources, and the preparation of coherent and objective policies, will become a necessary part of life for the public and voluntary sector.

Figure 2.1 illustrates the pattern of organisational development, from national bodies down to locally based voluntary organisations. At each level there is delegation of responsibility for the provision of services. National organisations function at national and international level whereas regional or county associations have by definition a more local perspective. The tendency in British sport is for the national focus to be on elite performance and major events. To illustrate the emphasis, for example, towards non-elite participants, organisations at a local level have powers delegated by the governing body to provide a sports service. Where elite performers become involved they may have an affiliation to a local club but they will also be expected to contribute to a sport at a higher level. Although the figure explains a delegated hierarchical approach not all sports match this profile exactly. The definition of an organisational structure at national, regional and local levels is basically accurate. Grant

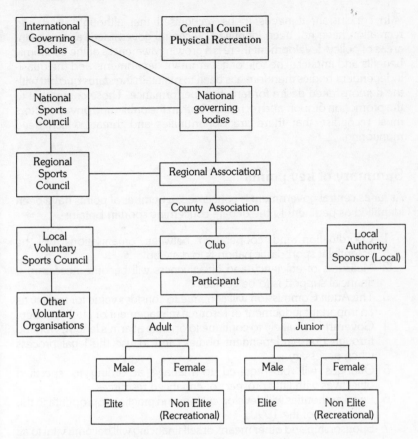

Figure 2.1 The organisation of sport and recreation

aid for appropriate activity tends to be awarded at the level for which the money will be used. The management of that money will then rest with the most suitable organisation.

Government acknowledges that sport, particularly in the voluntary sector, relies on enormous amounts of members' goodwill. There may well come a time when the voluntary sector gains greater recognition for its contribution to British culture. Issues involving central government that cause concern to the voluntary sector include:

- the effect of compulsory competitive tendering on the provision of appropriately priced facilities
- the loss of playing field space to developers
- the payment of Corporation Tax
- the effect of National Non-Domestic Rates on voluntary sports clubs
- the need to cater for young people and those who may be disadvantaged
- the ability to recruit and train volunteers into positions of authority

In conclusion, it needs to be recognised that although sport and recreation have not been identified by central government as important areas of policy development there is a growing awareness of the economic benefits and impact. The role of government departments and the quasi-independent bodies therefore has been to maintain the *status quo* but with the demonstrated desire for targets of performance. Those committed to the promotion of sport and recreation both in the public and private sectors must recognise that there are opportunities and threats which need monitoring.

Summary of key points

As far as central government is concerned, a number of points have been identified as pertinent to the debate concerning sport in Britain:

1 Coordination and cooperation between organisations will be essential if sport participation is to develop.
2 Measures of efficiency and effectiveness will become necessary if financial support is to be gained.
3 The Audit Commission will continue to consider value for money as an important judgement of resource management of public money.
4 Government is likely to continue to operate at arm's length, working through quasi-independent bodies, and to use the legal process when necessary.
5 Quangos will be required to manage according to specified objectives with little prospect of enhanced resources.
6 Local authorities will develop custom and practice appropriate to the constraints of the 1990s.
7 Sponsorship and other means of self financing will become vital to all sports organisations.
8 The market will operate as an important factor on what facilities and opportunities are needed.

There are a number of issues that are of direct relevance to managers. With an increasing emphasis being placed on resource management, the government has made it clear that market forces will play a greater role in the management of public buildings. Although CCT and contract management will contribute to this shift in emphasis managers themselves can expect greater flexibility, increased responsibility and measures of performance to determine their professional lives.

References

1 Education Reform Act 1988. HMSO, London.
2 Lord Justice Taylor 1989 *The Hillsborough Stadium Disaster, Final Report.* HMSO, London.
3 House of Lords Report Select Committee 1973 *Sport and Recreation,* HMSO, London.

4 White Paper Command Paper 6200: 1975 *Sport and Recreation*. HMSO, London.
5 Department of Education and Science 1991 *Sport and Active Recreation*. HMSO, London.

Further reading

The CCPR Annual Reports.

Central Office of Information Britain 1988 *An Official Handbook*. HMSO, London.

Coalter, F., Long, J. and Duffield, B. 1986 *Rationale for Public Sector Investment in Leisure*. The Sports Council, London.

The Henley Centre for Forecasting 1986 *The Economic Impact and Importance of Sport in the United Kingdom*, The Sports Council, London.

The Sports Council 1983 *Structure Function and Aims. Rationale for Public Sector Investment in Leisure*.

John Stewart and Gerry Stoker (editors) The Future of local Government 1989. Macmillan.

George Torkildson 1992 *Leisure and Recreation Management*, Third Edition. Spon/E & F Spon.

The Sports Council 1992 *Sport in the Nineties – New Horizons*.

Chris Gratton and Peter Taylor 1991 *Government and the Economics of Sport*. Longman.

National Curriculum Council 1991 *National Curriculum Council Report for Physical Education*.

3 Local government

Introduction

Democratically elected local authorities are responsible for the provision of a wide range of public services. The levels of local authority involvement and expenditure have increased during the post war years although central government has sought to constrain the growth of spending during the 1980s and 1990s. Central and local government are elected authorities each assuming a legal responsibility to deliver determined services. Local authorities, their elected members and officers, derive their powers from central government and in the performance of their duties are regulated by the law and a trend towards increasing central control.

The need for public money to be used effectively and efficiently has been a significant influence on local authorities in recent years. An independent Audit Commission monitors local government spending in England and Wales. Legislation introduced to encourage competition in the provision of local services has also influenced the development and delivery of a number of services, including sport and recreation.

Parliament confers powers and responsibilities on local authorities while appropriate ministers exercise their powers of supervision. In the case of sport and recreation in local authorities it is the Department of National Heritage that performs the most important role.

England and Wales is divided into 53 counties and 369 districts. With the exception of six metropolitan counties, each county and district elect unpaid councillors to a council. Counties and districts provide wide ranging services with the counties tending to focus on services such as planning, highways, police, refuse disposal and the fire service. Education, libraries and social services are also functions of the non-metropolitan counties. District authorities carry out local responsibilities including environmental health, housing and decision on planning applications.

The power of counties and districts to provide recreation and leisure services is concurrent although the reality is that local agreements determine specific areas of responsibility and provision. Whereas certain legislative powers confer a mandatory responsibility on local authorities, the provision of leisure services, including sport and recreation, is a permissive function. Education is a mandatory function of the appropriate local authority.

Within the metropolitan counties the district councils are responsible for all the services excepting the police, the fire service and public transport. It is in the metropolitan districts that we also find some of the larger recreation and leisure departments of England and Wales.

Greater London enjoys a separate relationship with central government. Since 1986 many of the functions previously carried out by the Greater London Council have been transferred to the London boroughs and metropolitan district councils. A number of services which cover wider areas are run by joint authorities. In inner London education was administered by the Inner London Education Authority until the Education Reform Act of 1988 required the inner London boroughs to assume responsibility. Responsibility for passenger transport lies with London Regional Transport. However London's metropolitan police force is directly responsible to the Home Secretary.

At a third level of local government, parish councils, in rural districts, represent local opinions though they can only exercise limited powers.

Scotland has a two-tier system based on nine regions and 53 districts, each with an elected council. In Northern Ireland 26 district councils are responsible for certain local services although central government maintains control through statutory bodies over such major services as education and libraries, health and social services.

Local authorities employ officers or staff to support the elected members in the effective delivery of local services. There is considerable freedom to organise local authority departments and staff teams although it is normal for a system of committees to oversee the development and operation of individual departments. With nearly three million people employed by local authorities in Great Britain they do represent a significant service.

In order to deliver the range of required services local authority finances are primarily raised from three sources: the Council Tax, National Non Domestic Rates (NNDR), and a grant from central government called the Revenue Support Grant (RSG). Additional income is derived from charges for services including housing rents, facility hire and admission to local authority run buildings including sports and recreation amenities.

As legal entities local authorities operate as corporate bodies, able to enter into contracts, sue or be sued and with the guarantee of perpetual succession.

Local authorities sport and recreation provision

Within the three tiered structure in England and Wales it is the counties and districts that exercise the greatest influence through mandatory and permissive powers. However, in focusing on local government it is important to recognise that over recent years there has been a fragmentation of service delivery. Local authorities increasingly share service delivery with a range of other organisations. The commitment of central government to competition and in particular to compulsory competitive tendering in the management of local authority sports and leisure facilities has brought about one of the most significant changes in the industry.

Education facilities

Education facilities are managed in England and Wales by the non metropolitan counties or, in the case of metropolitan areas, by the districts themselves. It is with these local education authorities in mind that the far reaching effects of the 1988 Education Reform Act presents issues concerning facility management which are wider than the inclusion and operation of sport and recreation programmes. This section seeks to highlight the more important sports related interests and how they may develop during the 1990s. Although this will include reference to the Act there are issues which go beyond the Act itself.

School sport, through the national curriculum in physical education and in extra curricular activity, has a considerable influence on sports participation in the United Kingdom. Wider community use of education facilities also makes a significant contribution to sport and recreation provision. Local education authorities are a vital link in the total pattern of sports development. The 1988 Education Reform Act[1] and the Local Management of Schools (LMS) appear to have changed that role; the effects of this will be seen both in short term profiles of participation and in long term development programmes for individual sports.

The time to be spent on physical education as a core subject within the National Curriculum must reach a minimum level of total curriculum time, but this highlights a concern that pressure from other examinable subjects, and their core time, plus the risk of accepting the minimum as standard, may place unacceptable limits on the quantity and quality of sport education in schools. Teachers themselves have played a valuable part in promoting sports participation and excellence. Indeed their contribution to representative sports including the performance of school teams, elite squads, county and national programmes has acted as encouragement to many children throughout the education system.

However the teachers' industrial dispute of the mid 1980s may have damaged both short and long term prospects for our school sport culture. Although other sports developments may alleviate the loss in the long term, there has been a diminution of school sports programmes. Extra curricular activity has been reduced which consequently places the onus on clubs, governing bodies, even local authority recreation departments to make good the lost opportunities.

The introduction and development of the National Curriculum in physical education promises a more objective and consistent presentation of the subject. A new repectability perhaps. Indeed it may also contribute towards a regard for health, fitness and an active lifestyle. However the prospect of increased work loads for teachers, in the preparation and assessment of coursework, could jeopardise time previously available for extra curricular programmes and competitive sport. There is also the risk of reducing the quality of a limited number of disciplines offered within the physical education syllabus by the need to cover a more wide ranging diet of physical activity; including those activities where the teacher may not be particularly well qualified.

Opening up wider usage of education facilities has been a matter. of debate since the Wolfenden Report[2] in 1960. Although dual use and joint provision schemes have provided greater access to sport, two related issues remain. Community use of education facilities is by no means as extensive as it might be. The development of agreed policies and procedures, determining management structures and making the necessary investment, has not always been easy for local authorities. As schools and the local education authorities consider management strategies for the rest of the 1990s the need for adequate resources remains a key issue. To sell off playing fields surplus to current needs could realise, at development prices, substantial sums of money. The demographic downturn of the late 1980s and early 1990s has potential, therefore, to rationalise the loss of educational sports amenity for all time. Education authorities could lose their influence over the quality and quantity of provision of facilities and programmes for those wishing to participate in sport.

One central feature of the 1988 Education Reform Act is the recognition by central government that parents should have a greater influence in the management of their schools. Under certain circumstances, and with the support of parents, school governors are being encouraged to apply to the Secretary of State for grant maintained status and as such to move away from, or opt out of, local authority ownership and control. One anxiety amongst educationists points to the prospect of certain schools determining a more selective intake and a redefinition of values and priorities. If this is an area of uncertainty the local management of schools (LMS) is a reality. From April 1990 schools assumed responsibility for managing their budgets. It is argued that this encourages greater accountability to parents and the community. The extent to which a school encourages an extra curricular programme will be guided by cost implications and parental attitudes. Local Management of Schools places additional pressure on headteachers and governors to raise income through greater use of their facilities. It also suggests that current users should pay a hire charge or fee that actually reflects the real cost of provision plus a contribution to the school budget. Opportunities to hire school facilities should increase but this may be at a price which reduces either the quantity or the quality of the sport programme. However, there certainly remains scope for increasing public use of school facilities and for contributing to community sport.

Local authority education departments face a diminished role in sport and recreation provision through the 1990s but they do retain the ability and the opportunity to foster partnerships and to promote the enhancement of educational values and standards. The problem faced by

LEAs is that with reduced power, and the limitations of a finite budget, they lack the resources to service schools as they might wish. It seems likely that variations in provision will emerge as headteachers and governors develop their appreciation of LMS, and the education authorities redefine their role and contribution to the community.

Partnerships, cooperation and collaboration between various agencies, will by force of circumstance become increasingly important if standards of performance are to improve. As a result of changes in local authority responsibility for the management of schools, the consequence of financial constraints on the local management of schools, schools electing grant maintained status and the impact of the National Curriculum on teaching physical education, partners have become essential if sport beyond the physical education programme is to prosper. Many leisure departments, having gone to tender and with contracts awarded for the management of leisure facilities, have elected to retain the responsibility for sport development within the client section. As the case study at the end of this chapter illustrates in many areas there has been a shift of responsibility for extra curricular and competitive sport towards the local authority leisure services department. The impact of sport development officers working for their governing bodies is considered in more detail in Chapter 6 but they have also had an impact on school sport.

Sport and recreation departments

Although the counties and districts in England and Wales enjoy the opportunity to provide sport and recreation facilities and programmes there is a tremendous variety in terms of what they actually do.

Just as there is no consistency in the provision of facilities for sport and recreation, so there is tremendous variety in the departmental structures that administer the programmes.

Indeed there have been engineers departments administering sport and recreation, a model that dates back to when swimming pool provision dominated supply and engineers managed the pools. Departmental titles such as, Recreation and Leisure, Sport and Recreation, Leisure and Tourism, Economic Development and Leisure illustrate the current diversity and the different emphasis.

Managing even a small local authority can be a complex matter requiring coordination of many services and a budget of millions of pounds. Sport or recreation managers are required to work at two levels:

1 The administration of senior staff supervising programmes and subordinates.
2 Dealing with the political dimension, the elected members, and the delivery of policies across a number of departments.

Local authority departments which focus on sport and recreation, and relying on permissive powers to provide services, have evolved contrasting styles. Counties tend to take a wider view of their responsibilities while district councils and metropolitan districts take a more parochial view of their role in sport and recreation. Departments have been responsible for planning, delivering and evaluating programmes, approved by councillors and the appropriate committees, which best reflect the interests of the electorate.

Judging what is good for a community is a political activity. Finite resource allocation is therefore made on the basis of a political determination of local need although local authorities can only act using powers the law has given them. Competition for service delivery stimulates a different approach to service provision. Even where local authorities continue to manage their own facilities, a necessary separation of responsibilities between the client and the contractor roles has effected a more fundamental change. A closer relationship between paying for and receiving a service encourages the demand for high quality and effective management performance.

There are no agreed standards of provision for sport and recreation, no common approaches to facility development and a tremendous variety of approaches by local authorities. The introduction of compulsory competitive tendering and contract management has also confirmed two factors, firstly that government through Parliament has the power to effect change, and secondly that local authorities would prefer local control and the continuance of permissive powers.

Local government measures of performance

In the 1970s and 1980s there was a significant increase in facility provision and the opportunity to participate. New sports motivation schemes accompanied diversification in facility provision, including artificial pitches and leisure pools, which began to cater for increased demand for recreational activity and sport.

There remain fundamental differences of political opinion concerning the role of local government in sport and recreation. In a mixed UK leisure economy, where leisure is served by both public and private sectors, through commercial provision and subsidies to users, the character of public sector investment needs to be defined. Local authorities perform an enabling role and ensure that opportunities to participate are identified. Previously able to build facilities and manage them, or build and contract out the management, local authorities are now required to adopt a competitive approach to facility management and programme development. Priorities may be forced to change just as needs and target groups come under pressure from alternative more cost effective strategies.

The implications for organisations and managers will become widespread. In a profession where there is an emerging identity and coherence, a heavy responsibility rests with organisations like the Institute of Leisure and Amenity Management to encourage consistency, standards of performance and cooperation amongst managers in the public and private sectors.

Local authorities will have to operate in an environment where leisure needs will be continually redefined. Commercial activity will continue to grow thus exercising a keen influence on local provision and management. Social policies will be adjusted to reflect changing political and economic priorities.

The development of policies and resources for disadvantaged groups should remain a consideration for local authorities. Selective target marketing will be necessary if objectives are to be satisfied.

Facility provision, originally designed specifically for sport, has more recently been characterised by the development of leisure amenities. Careful consideration now needs to be given regarding design concepts which cater for both the fun or entertainment element and the need to develop performance and excellence in sport.

Education and training of staff has largely been undervalued in the local authority sector. The opportunities for sports development demand better trained staff. In house training schemes, cooperation between neighbouring authorities, partnerships with further and higher education and a greater commitment to education and training will become increasingly important.

Clearly defined written social and economic objectives, which conform with corporate goals, are required for every recreation facility or sport programme. Performance then needs to be measured against the satisfaction of those social and economic objectives within a defined period of time. The commercial sector is normally required to work towards financial targets and economic measures of performance. Specification documents for compulsory competitive tendering should provide appropriate detail on these factors.

Information systems designed to service the needs of management, with up to date appropriately detailed data, are essential if managers are to control, evaluate or review programmes of work. Too little or too much information offered too late, perhaps without explanation, does not help the manager to improve efficiency or effectiveness. Decision making often has to occur within a limited period of time. Local authority managers, acting as contractors, need to work with flexibility and the ability to react quickly to situations if they are to succeed.

Customer care remains at the centre of any service industry. Sport and recreation within the public sector is no exception to this. All staff from manager down must appreciate the needs of consumers. Those with the greatest contact with the public are more likely to require regular training and awareness programmes.

Competition for local authority services

The encouragement of competition for local authority contracts is based on the need or the ability to produce a service which enjoys consumer demand. The introduction of competitive tendering was designed to save public money by encouraging more efficient management of sports and recreation facilities. Local authorities acting as clients become demanding customers; they are likely to choose activities and carefully monitor programmes. Any local authority, or client, will want to measure the outcome of a contractor's work and insist on measures of quantity and quality control. Before going on to examine the market led approach, and CCT in particular, it is important to confirm that there has indeed been a role for the private sector in local government contracts although the situation has varied between authorities. During the years 1981-1988, 131 councils contracted out 100 million of work saving millions of pounds. Indeed compulsory competitive tendering is not new to local authorities. The Local Government Planning and Land Act of 1980 introduced compulsory competitive tendering in the construction and maintenance of buildings and highways.

Local Government Act, 1988[3]

The increased emphasis on accountability to central government and to the community it serves is likely to change the face of local government through the 1990s. Compulsory competitive tendering is only one aspect of a piece of legislation that has far reaching implications. Essentially the Act is a challenge to local representative democracy and is based on the underlying argument that some local authorities spend too much money or have had too much power. In light of the 1988 Local Government Act there has been fundamental redefinition of the role of local government.

Changes to local government finance took place in April 1990 with the introduction of:

1 Community Charge (or Poll Tax).
   The Community Charge failed to gain popular or political support, was difficult and expensive to administer and was replaced in 1993 by the Council Tax; a tax based on the value of a property.
2 National Non Domestic Rates (NNDR).
3 Revenue Support Grant (RSG).

National Non Domestic Rates on all non-domestic properties, including sports and recreation facilities, are determined and allocated to local authorities, by central government, but local authorities administer and collect the tax. In terms of local authority income derived from these sources, the Council Tax will contribute 25 per cent, as will the NNDR with the Revenue Support Grant bringing the remaining 50 per cent. Therefore local authorities will be responsible for influencing only 25 per cent of their total income. About 75 per cent of local authority income will come from central government in the form of National Non Domestic Rates and Revenue Support Grant thus spreading the load and widening accountability, but with 75 per cent of income coming in this way there is a reduction in local authority power.

The underlying ambition of central government is a movement towards letting the market determine new ways of providing local authority services, reducing the power of local authorities, the trades union and collective bargaining.

Compulsory competitive tendering (CCT)

One dimension of the 1988 Local Government Act, the introduction of CCT in sport and recreation management has had a considerable impact on local authorities. Indeed the publication of a Parliamentary Order in October 1989 required local authorities to submit the management of all sport and leisure facilities to competitive tender by 1993. Every local authority-owned sports centre or leisure centre has been subjected to CCT unless they belong to an educational institution or are extensively used by educational institutions. Difficulties exist over certain terms and conditions especially in understanding joint provision and dual use. The latest dates by which CCT was implemented in England and Wales were:

1st January 1992	35%
1st August 199	270%
1st January 1993	100%

(Contract periods are 4-6 years).

Wales was included but with a different timetable. Facilities which do not cost more than 100,000 have been exempt.

Local authorities, should they choose to compete with others to manage facilities, will be required to adopt clearly defined management strategies. Although the role of contractor will be open to competition, local authorities retain the client responsibility. It was therefore their task to draw up the precise specifications for managing all elements of the service, and to do so ahead of time for all facilities to go to tender together. Since there has been an element of local authority contracting out in the leisure sector the process is not entirely unfamiliar. The difference between previous practice and the demands of CCT were that there was no choice for local authorities; services had to go to tender. Local authorities have lost the ability to exercise the power to manage, and the private sector is encouraged to compete for contracts with cost effective operational systems.

Managing sports and leisure facilities

Managing sports and leisure facilities includes:

- providing instruction in the sport or other physical recreational activity provided
- supervising the sport or activity
- hiring out equipment for use at the facility

- catering
- providing refreshments
- marketing and promoting the facility
- taking bookings
- collecting and accounting for fees and charges
- assuming responsibility for heating, lighting and other service charges in relation to the facility
- making the facility secure
- cleaning and properly maintaining the facility (except for the external structures of buildings).

The Secretary of State has the power to amend or extend this list. It is not intended to be exhaustive. Local authorities retained some powers, including the discretion to specify pricing, admission and opening hours in their tender documents. These conditions were not to encourage anti-competitive practice. Financial objectives were specified when an authority won a contract with its in-house staff.

Local authorities needed to prepare for competitive tendering through:

1 The preparation of detailed strategic plans which considered the full range of sport and recreation services.
2 The identification of a role for each facility, or group of facilities, in satisfying specific priorities.
3 The recognition of a need for an appropriate balanced programme in each community. This required the establishment of policies for target groups, incorporating pricing, the role of local voluntary sports clubs, and the development of excellence.

One of the problems faced by many local authorities is that they needed to prepare these important strategy documents on up to date accurate information based on the communities they serve. For plans to succeed they needed to focus on an objective assessment of performance prior to the preparation of tender specifications. Some accuracy was required regarding profiles, consumer satisfaction, community needs, disadvantaged groups and effective marketing.

Seeking value for money suggests quality and not just quantity and recognises that value, despite being a subjective assessment, is an important dimension of any leisure service.

The cost of providing a local authority service can only be truly compared with the private sector if measures of performance are compared like with like. It is unlikely that the conditions of employment experienced before CCT will bear comparison to those in the 1990s. In order that local authorities could compete for their own contracts, direct labour organisations, working within any authority, needed to become flexible and adaptable even if this resulted in a diminution or change in the quality of work conditions.

Certainly local authorities now have a regard for the quality of provision and the projected income/profit figures resulting from the award of any contract.

Local authority sports and recreation facilities are not going to become profit making enterprises, generating an acceptable return on investment, unless they were designed and built for that purpose. Since most facilities are provided to cater for community needs, and they include consideration for disadvantaged groups, it is unlikely that profit could ever be the prime motive. Financial targets are necessary in any business environment but they must be realistic. Measures of performance, including ratio analysis, need to profile those aspects which are specific to a community based service sector industry. However the variability of strategy documents makes the exercise of identifying and measuring performance indicators a complicated matter. In fact locally derived parameters make such an exercise very difficult to detail.

Local authorities seeking to win contracts needed to re-organise departmental structures so that 'a distance' was created between those who were clients and those who would become contractors. It follows that both sides needed to plan and prepare carefully. Satisfactory service provision follows the preparation of sound strategic arguments. Coordinated planning and the evaluation of management programmes can generate a new outlook and role for local authorities. The private sector and the public sector can provide effective partnerships but it requires the determination to succeed.

Governing bodies of sport which depend on the use of local authority facilities, in particular the Amateur Swimming Association (ASA) and the British Athletics Federation (BAF),[4] (previously the AAA) were concerned at the possible disruption in the use of facilities. The cost implications of redesigned pricing policies were also considered a significant threat by these governing bodies. Provision for club use of a facility (by any sport) has become an important matter for any strategy document to determine.

Quality systems

Total quality management (TQM) and the application of quality systems through BS5750 became a live issue as client teams have sought means whereby they could be assured a quality service and the delivery of acceptable standards by the contractor.[5] The introduction of a quality system through BS5750 is just one stage in the longer term process of attaining total quality management. Although this chapter is not the place for a lengthy discourse on TQM or BS5750 it is important for the reader to recognise that CCT contributed to the development of a systematic preparation of specifications which provided the framework around which management could determine the standard of service required. Written statements on quality policy, the determination of all employees responsibility towards achieving quality, the appointment of a quality officer and the provision of a review mechanism are all management responsibilities built into BS5750.

Local government re-organisation

The process of local government re-organisation has not ceased with the competitive tendering process; it continues until 1998 when the last of the new local authorities are established. A National Commission began its work in 1992 examining the various options for the future of local government. The Commission is reviewing the two tier system of county and district councils to see whether a unitary system would better suit the needs of local communities in a cost effective system of local management. With the review being undertaken in five stages, and each stage expected to last eight to 16 months, the new authorities begin to take effect from 1994. Essentially the task for the Commission is to define the preferred unitary authority system and how it would function most effectively and efficiently, taking account of expressed preferences. As one might imagine the county and the district authorities find themselves in a competitive situation where ultimately one authority may disappear altogether, leaving one level of local government responsible for the services previously managed by the two tier system. The implications for local services, including the provision of sport and recreation, are considerable, but they are very much dependent on the outcome to the Commission's work, the preferred system of local government and the nature of the management structure that replaces the current system.

Summary of key points

1 Local authorities have played an important role in the development of sport and recreation. Both education and recreation departments, in contributing facilities and opportunities to participate, have also been instrumental in enabling the voluntary sector to benefit. The particularly rapid development of facilities during the 1970s was matched by a growth of local authority influence in sport provision.

2 The 1980s witnessed attempts by central government to curb local authority spending and power. Although facility developments continued, and the contribution of appropriate departments remained significant, the winds of change were beginning to blow. Schools participation in competitive and recreational sports did not emerge from the 1980s unscathed, nor did the local authority recreation departments escape the attention of central government. The Education Reform Act and the Local Government Act mark 1988 as a time when the process of change gathered pace.

3 Although critics of central government may not admire the motivation behind the changes to local government, there are others who see the opportunities for sport and recreation, particularly since the 1990s are seen to be a time of growth for the leisure industries.

4 The underlying trend will be for local authorities to move towards an executive style of management. Elected members will exert their

influence over planning and control rather than all aspects of service delivery.

5   The economics of market forces will provide an increasingly important dimension in programme development. Pressure on land space and the real loss of playing field provision is just one illustration of what can happen.

6   Accountability for resource utilisation has become a major issue in local government. Managers will increasingly be required to measure results against agreed objectives or targets.

7   The sport and recreation industry evolved rapidly with local government taking a key responsibility in the 1970s and 1980s. Subsequently compulsory competitive tendering has provided a new set of relationships for local authorities in the 1990s. The implementation of a unitary system of local authorities will maintain the process of local government reform and place at risk both the level and quality of sport and recreation provision.

Case study: City of Sunderland; sport development

Introduction

Local authorities can and have responded in a variety of ways following the impact of recent legislation and spending constraints. The development of partnerships, collaborative ventures and cooperation between agencies have all been identified as the most likely ways of continuing to improve the provision of local services in sport and recreation.

The City of Sunderland and the Department of Leisure Services have responded to a variety of opportunities to promote sport and recreation and have done so through the efforts of their client division. This case study is not concerned with the contract division's management of the facilities following CCT; it considers the potential and real impact of a dynamic client division determined to realise new projects using a variety of partners, associated agencies, grant aiding organisations, a professional sports club and industrial sponsorship.

Within the client division there is a development section devoted to the preparation and implementation of strategic and policy goals in sports development. Currently the section has responsibility for the delivery of development plans in tennis, swimming, football, hockey, basketball, table tennis, netball, fitness, rugby union and cycling. Specific plans for each of these sports have or are being prepared to enable the achievement of strategic plans and policy statements. The policy statements refer to specific target groups or sensitive areas of interest. These include young people, women, people with disabilities, ethnic groups, community recreation, centres of excellence, countryside issues, water sports and fishing. All documents, policies and plans focus on a period to the year 2000.

The section itself is divided into four elements each of which may overlap with another depending on the nature of a given programme. The elements within the section are facility development, new projects, sports development and special events. The head of development, a principal officer, chairs all working groups and the five client development officers each have responsibility for a number of sports and specific policies. In fact the five are likely to undertake responsibilities in each of the four main areas of work. One client development officer has a specific responsibility for netball, aerobics/fitness, champion coaching, ethnic groups, women, and special needs. The client development officers use support staff and they may have an assistant depending on the nature of the project or event. In addition there are two events officers and a promotion officer within the section. The authority also employs some 150 coaches, about half of which work in football and swimming.

Partnerships

The development section is involved with a wide variety of organisations including the Department of Environment regarding land reclamation and City Challenge, the European Social Fund for a scheme targeted at disadvantaged groups, Sunderland FC and a community based football development scheme and the Sports Council with work associated with regional priorities identified within the focus sports or within the regional strategy. In addition to the above list there are partners committed to the specific work taking in the local education authority, local schools, sports clubs, Sunderland Sports Council (a voluntary group), Sunderland Coaches Association, charitable trusts, commercial leisure operators, and industrial sponsors.

The nature of any partnership will depend on the type of activity, the availability of grant aid or sponsorship, the physical input of personnel from sports clubs, schools and other organisations plus those members of the community who will most benefit from the added provision of sport and recreation.

Ultimately the success of any scheme or project will depend on the satisfaction of strategic and policy goals in partnership, the ability to offer staffing and equipment resources and the delivery of quality in achieving customer satisfaction.

Like many major local authorities Sunderland also has a budget which is committed to grant aiding community based projects. The money, some 25,000 in 1993, is awarded to clubs and organisations that satisfy certain objectives including personal performance advancement, club development grant, coach/instructor education and special needs. The receipt of a grant is dependent upon the applicant presenting an application which identifies how the grant will assist in the achievement of individual or organisational goals.

Examples of sport development

To illustrate the nature of the development section's work examples have been taken from each of the four main areas of activity. Under facility development there are a number of programmes including: the Sunderland Ski Centre, incorporating a significant extension to the dry ski slope at Silksworth; a Cyclo-cross track at Hetton Lyons and a separate 1.8 km closed road circuit.

New projects involve City Challenge, the European Social Fund, and the establishment of the Coaches Association. The City Challenge programme embodies an enhanced version of Action Sport involving local schools from the urban community and focusing on improving facilities and coaching basketball, tennis and netball. The activities will be supported by coaches and equipment with the City Challenge moneys also funding the rehabilitation of outdoor playing facilities.

The development section also has plans to build an international standard Go Kart Track. Agreements have already been forged with a developer and following land-fill requirements at a local quarry the project will move ahead. The Sports Council has supported with grant aid the appointment of a community use awareness officer to promote better use of school sports facilities.

The sports development work addresses the priorities identified in the written plans and represents an ongoing programme of activity, for example every ten weeks 2,500 people are recruited to a total of ten venues for a swimming course.

Working with partners such as Sunderland FC and the Footballers Further Educational Vocational and Training Society (FFEVTS) the section presents a local scheme designed to provide training to individuals on YTS and Employment Action. Football coaching courses are also offered to 7-16 year olds across a geographical area measuring nearly 100 miles by 50 miles; from Berwick in the north to Hexham in the west. A classroom project based at the professional club encourages each school in the area to spend one day per year at the club. In addition the club makes 500 tickets available for local schools to attend home matches. The club and the development section have established a highly creditable link between themselves and the local community.

A Champion Coaching blueprint is designed to promote youth sport coaching for performance motivated children. The provision of quality after school coaching opportunities for children of 11-14 years of age is all based within the local community. Champion Coaching is a national scheme, designed by the National Coaching Foundation, supported by the Sports Council, and includes 14 sports. The cost of the coaching programme is met by a 33 per cent grant and 67 per cent fees and charges. Sunderland have addressed their needs through the work of a Youth Sport Manager and a Youth Sport Advisory Group acting as a think tank, made up of representatives from the NCF, the Sports Council, the P.E. Adviser for Sunderland, the respective chairpersons to the local Sports Council, the Coaches Association and the Secondary Head Teachers Association. Each sport has a sports development group working to agreed aims and specific objectives.

The special events programme includes 19 events during 1993-1994, varying in size and invariably involving local sports associations or clubs. A bowling competition for some 400-500 bowlers is organised in association with the local bowling association and a tennis event is managed in partnership with Durham and Cleveland LTA. Each of the 19 events requires a small planning team. The most prestigious event is perhaps the annual International Football Festival, now held three times during the summer and sponsored in 1992 by Cowies. It is a competition which attracts leading teams from Europe and South America as well as top British clubs, attracting over 40,000 spectators. There are competitions in the age categories under 16 and under 19, a seven-a-side competition for younger children, a national ladies competition and a competition for people with a disability.

Many of the activities and developments profiled would not take place without the active support of key agencies. The development section therefore plays a crucial role in facilitating the implementation of an extensive programme. The financial constraints of local authority activity are also offset by the grants and physical support that many offer to the development section. Indeed each of the many activities that takes place has its own cost centre, an appreciation of local authority input and targets for grant aid, sponsorship, fees and charges.

References

1 The Education Reform Act 1988. HMSO, London.
2 The Wolfenden Committee on Sport 1960 *Sport and the Community.* HMSO, London.
3 Local Government Act 1988. HMSO, London.
4 Annual Reports for AAA's and ASA 1988.
5 Peter Mills (Editor) 1992 *Quality in the Leisure Industry.* Longman.

Further reading

Annual Reports of Governing Bodies of Sport.
The Chartered Institute of Public Finance and Accountancy Annual Publication *Charges for Leisure Services.* CIPFA.
Coalter, F., Long, J. and Duffield, B. 1986 *Rationale for Public Sector Investment in Leisure.* The Sports Council, London.
Glyptis, S. and Pack, C. 1988 *Study 31: Local Authority Sport Provision for the Unemployed.* The Sports Council, London.

Gratton, C and Taylor, P. 1991 *Government and Economics of Sport.* Longman.

Gratton, C. and Taylor, P. 1992 *Economics of Leisure Services Management.* Longman/ILAM.

Houlihan, B. 1991 *The Government and Politics of Sport* Routledge.

School Sport Forum, 1988 *Sport and Young People: Partnership and Action.* The Sports Council, London.

Sport in the Community: Into the 90s 1988. The Sports Council, London.

Stewart, J. & Stoker, G. (eds) 1989 *The Future of local Government.* Macmillan.

The Sports Council Annual Reports.

1988 Competitive Tendering, Where do we go from here? The Sports Council, London. *Rationale for Public Sector Investment in Leisure.*

Torkildsen, G. 1992 *Leisure and Recreation Managment* Third Edition. Spon/E & F N Spon.

4 The Sports Council

Introduction

Although central government does not seek to exercise direct power and control over sport and recreation in the UK, it is generally acknowledged that it plays an influential role. The manner in which sports organisations are encouraged, and the contribution that central government makes, is largely measured through the work of local authorities and quasi-independent organisations. A more overt interest in sport and recreation by central government has been increasingly evident over the last twenty or so years.

Following a detailed examination of sport and recreation, a move that was inspired by the CCPR, the Wolfenden Committee Report, *Sport in the Community* was published in 1960.[1] An independent committee, it sought to recommend to statutory and voluntary bodies what action was required regarding sports and outdoor activities. It was also felt that a wide ranging response to its recommendations was necessary.

The early years

After the formation of an Advisory Sports Council in 1965 and the establishment of an executive body in 1972, an attempt was made to quantify needs through the two Provision for Sport reports, in 1972 and 1973.[2] With the assistance of voluntary bodies and local authorities, including LEA's, an attempt was made to determine the need for facilities and the promotion of participation. Targets were established and published in Sport in the Seventies.[3] Financial investment was considered important if the targets were to be met. Although central funding remained limited, local authorities invested heavily in sport during the early and mid 1970s. Facilities for sport improved significantly. Provision was made possible because local government re-organisation in 1974 resulted in outgoing councils spending, and because large sport, recreation or leisure departments were formed at local authority level.

Following the House of Lords Select Committee[4] consideration of sport and recreation a White Paper Sport and Recreation[5], was debated one year later. Priorities based on socio-economic need and performance were subsequently to become areas of special interest to the Sports Council. In particular, inner cities, excellence, community-based schemes and the encouragement of sponsorship were highlighted. The 1970s represented a time when the nation began to recognise priorities for sport.

The White Paper clearly endorsed the view that subsidies for recreation were appropriate. Indeed, the government DNH accepted that recreation should be regarded as one of the community's everyday needs and that provision for it is part of the general fabric of social services.[5]

Certain benefits were seen to accrue from participation in sport and recreation.

1 Health benefits from taking exercise.
2 Positive (rather than negative or destructive) use of an individual's energy and time.
3 The wider benefits enjoyed through international success.

These three benefits remain as a consistent factor in central government's view of sport in British society.

As we move through the 1990s one further thought from the 1975 White Paper seems appropriate:

Where the community neglects its responsibilities for providing the individual with opportunities and choice in the provision of sport and recreational facilities, it will rarely escape the long-term consequences of this neglect. (Cmnd 6200)[5]

The establishment of a Sports Council

When established by Royal Charter in 1972 the Sports Council became the independent and executive body responsible for:

1 Fostering the knowledge and practice of sport and recreation among the public at large.
2 Providing facilities.
3 Building upon the work in this field of the Central Council of Physical Recreation and others.

Sports Councils for Scotland and Wales were also formed in 1972 with the Secretary of State for Scotland and the Secretary of State for Wales responsible for conferring functions and duties. There is no doubt that the Royal Charter provided an important role for the appropriate Minister of the Crown.

Sport and active recreation

The Department of National Heritage (DNH), through the Secretary of State, has responsibility for sport and recreation, and as such exercises the duty to promote or join any debate considering policies for sport.

Managing any sports organisation requires a clear view of objectives. Plans, however, must also be adaptable and flexible. From time to time opportunities or threats to the programme may determine some adjustment. Plans should not be carved in stone. They must be used simply as a means of achieving strategic goals. Regular evaluation of schedules, and of priorities, can provide new insights. The government announced its views on sport in the UK, in December 1991, with the publication of *Sport and Active Recreation*.[6] A document which provided an indication of the government's perception of the importance of sport in people's lives.

Known as the Minister's Review, *Sport and Active Recreation*, was published when responsibility for sport had only recently moved to the Department of Education from the Department of the Environment. This was not long before the function and the Sport and Recreation Division (SARD) moved to the newly created Department of National Heritage (DNH); offering cabinet status to the Secretary of State. At this stage it is worth noting that the government identified primary objectives for sport and recreation, in late 1991, as being:

1 To ensure that physical education takes its proper place in the school curriculum, and to ensure that pupils participate regularly in sport and physical exercise.
2 To promote physical exercise and participation in sport and active recreation by adults, giving support where appropriate to the provision of facilities and of opportunities for participation.
3 To help participants in sport to achieve higher standards of performance and to enable those with the potential to excel to do so
4 To promote better use of local authority and school sports facilities, and partnerships with the private sector in the provision and management of sports facilities.
5 To promote for people with disabilities and to encourage the greater integration of able-bodied and disabled people in sporting activities.
6 To promote fair play, supported by an effective, independent drug testing regime.
7 To promote the interests of UK sport internationally.

Given that the parent department at the time of publication was the DES, the interest in physical education is not surprising. The new factors, in terms of an official report indicating government priorities, were independent drug testing and the promotion of sport for people with disability (including the encouragement towards integration).

Otherwise the advertised aims of 1987 and 1991 were close to the views expressed in the 1975 White Paper;[7] little would appear to have changed. In fact, changes in emphasis and determining means of pursuing these aims have taken place. The Sports Council itself has been referred to as the government's principal adviser in the development and promotion of sport. With limited resources available for sport, some difficult decisions have to be made regarding the allocation of grant aid. Grant aid policies need to find a balance between encouraging participation and providing for excellence. The government in 1993 sees the Sports Council as providing the independent but accountable body responsible for providing appropriate assistance to sport in the UK.

Functions of the Sports Council

The Minister's review identified the required reforms to the existing structure of the UK Sports Council. The determination of final responsibilities takes effect from late 1993 when a number of changes will take place. In order to appreciate the nature of developments and how they relate to previous responsibilities we must acknowledge a historical background to the Sports Council and its activities.

The Royal Charter, awarded in 1972, gave the Sports Council certain powers which focused on an enabling role. Their responsibilities were based upon the need to develop, improve, encourage and support others in their provision and management of sports opportunities and facilities. Sport was felt by central government to contribute to social welfare, the enjoyment of leisure time and to the reputation of the country through international competitions.

In defining objectives for the Sports Council it was seen that the exercise of their responsibilities would also be through the encouragement of others to research and promote knowledge. Collaboration at an international level would further assist governing bodies and others to take advantage of these representative activities.

Financial support, through grants or loans, would be given to promote the ambitions of government and the Sports Council. Resources would be channelled to schemes which demonstrated compatibility with the objectives of the Sports Council and the government.

There was, and still is, a clear responsibility to central government for its actions although the need to cooperate with other organisations either pursuing similar goals, or interested in related matters, has remained central to the exercise of its functions.

The provision of facilities has been a function of the Sports Council although the reality has been largely focused on the support of others in facility development.

A reformed Sports Council

A UK Sports Commission assumed responsibility in 1993 for long-term strategic planning on matters of UK interest, the coordination of efforts to promote participation, the development and coordination of initiatives to promote higher standards of performance and excellence in sport at a UK level, collaboration with international bodies and the administration of grants or loans to achieve these objectives.[8]

The UK Commission is made up of a chairperson and ten members. Each home country has one member and in addition there is a representative from the British Sports Forum (comprising the CCPR, the BOA and the sports associations of Wales, Scotland, and Northern Ireland), the British Olympic Association (BOA), and four independent members appointed by the Secretary of State. The new UK body intends to be independent of individual home country offices.

The four Sports Councils, one for each country, are responsible for promoting participation, the development of foundational skills in sport, the promotion of performance and excellence, the encouragement of facility provision, the promotion of active recreation and the allocation of grant aid to implement these objectives.

In England there is a regional structure including offices and a secretariat to support the Regional Councils for Sport and Recreation (RCSR). The chairperson to these regions sits on the English Sports Council together with four independent members, a representative of the CCPR and a chairperson. The work of the Sports Council is to be primarily funded via grant aid from the Department of National Heritage. It is also an ambition of the DNH that an amount equivalent to 10 per cent of the regional budget should be raised from attracting private sector funding to support schemes meeting Sports Council objectives.

Scotland, Wales and Northern Ireland continue to have a responsibility to their respective Secretary's of State. It is unlike therefore that their work will be greatly affected by the re-organisation.

For purposes of clarity this chapter will focus on the Sports Council in England, both in considering the past and considering the future. Where appropriate specific reference will be made to another country within the UK.

Development issues

In determining a national strategy for sport the Sports Council has to acknowledge the influence of the contributing department, particularly the Sport and Recreation Division (SARD) and the definition of its own regional strategies.

Only then, and through effective communications, can the organisation develop its corporate plan. The implementation of such a plan largely depends on the efforts of others, particularly the national sports organisations, central services of the Sports Council and regional work programmes. The National Coaching Foundation (NCF), for example, has been seen as the coaching arm of the Sports Council, responsible for the delivery of an important part of the Sports Council's plan. The NCF's contribution to the development of coach education, in association with many other organisations, is likely to underpin the improvement of UK coach education during the 1990s. To achieve this the NCF requires support and encouragement from the Sports Council and others, both nationally and regionally.

An organisational structure for the Sports Council has to recognise the need for positive links between the centre and the infrastructure that delivers the programmes. Central services, finance, and management support are necessary as are the duties delegated from senior staff who maintain a coordinating and evaluation overview of the Sports Council work.

As a promotional body, the Sports Council is concerned with the development of participation in all sports and recreation. Most governing bodies have promotional and coaching award schemes, and certificates of competence are issued to their coaches. The Sports Council has assisted many of these governing bodies in the administration of these schemes. At national and regional level, the Sports Council cooperates with many agencies in promoting participation and improving standards, and in identifying regional priorities. Assistance is given, within the limitations of the amount of money available, towards the provision of recreational facilities sponsored by statutory, commercial and voluntary organisations. A scheme operates whereby loans may be available to local voluntary organisations. Regional participation grants are also provided to agencies seeking to increase participation.

The Sports Council is keenly involved in advising on the provision and management of recreation facilities, in cooperation with agencies such as the Regional Councils for Sport and Recreation, the Standing Conferences of Sport and Recreation, local authorities, district and local sports councils and voluntary bodies.

The independence of the Sports Council has been viewed as an attempt to move sport away from politics. If the Sports Council is to have more than just a regard to the Secretary of State's wishes, to what extent can the Council be seen as both independent and executive?

To be realistic HM Government has always had the opportunity to assume a strong central position in determining policies and programme emphasis. Furthermore it remains pertinent to a study of the Sports Council that 'the goalposts can be moved' by those who hold the highest authority.

Not only can government keenly influence the operation of the Sports Council, but no one should lose sight of the fact that the law of the land will always remain paramount. Competitive tendering legislation and changes in non domestic rating are examples of the ability of legislation to affect sport and recreation.

Sports Council strategies

It is generally recognised by central and local government, and the Sports Council, that there is much more that needs to be done for UK sport. At each level of performance resourcing is acknowledged as a critical element in determining future strategies. Central government has not identified provision for sport as a spending priority. Local government, having invested heavily through the 1970s and 1980s, is now faced with the consequence of compulsory competitive tendering of facilities, contract management, and continued constraints on capital and revenue spending.

Meanwhile the Sports Council continues to rely on grant aid from central government.

There are a number of ways of looking at the problems that arise. An examination of central and local government in sport is clearly important. So too must we consider the identification and satisfaction of Sports Council objectives. This will be achieved by reviewing previous Sports Council policies and practice including the strategy documents *Sport in the Community, Into the 90s, A strategy for Sport 1988-1993,*[9] and *Sport in the Nineties – New Horizons.*[10]

Prior to these publications came *Sport in the Community: The Next Ten Years*[11] which considered the development of sport in Britain (particularly through the 1970s) and identified priorities for 1983-1993. This document effectively leads to the others in determining a strategic approach. Fundamentally it carried the advice that sport must be understood and planned for against wider changes in society. During these ten years:

- there was a smaller school and teenage population, but more adults, many in smaller households
- population growth was concentrated on smaller towns, rural areas, and outer city rings, demanding up-graded or new sports facilities
- larger families, low income groups, and single person households in inner cities had special needs to be met
- there was more leisure time, (though its distribution is unclear), and high-levels of unemployment. Consequently, there was an increasing demand for leisure pursuits with sport being one of the most buoyant
- the relationship between increasing travel costs and patterns of participation needed to be monitored

Sporting participation grew in popularity and frequency. Broadly, participation in outdoor sport doubled in the 1960s and in indoor sport in the 1970s, when outdoor sport grew by a further 50 per cent. By 1980, 30 per cent were taking part in outdoor sport once a month or more often and 23 per cent in indoor sport regularly. This represented growth of 7.2 per cent and 6.1 per cent respectively in the three years since 1977. Participation had grown considerably amongst younger middle-aged men and women, and especially amongst skilled manual groups. But there were groups which were low in participation, house-wives, especially those with young children, semi and unskilled workers, people over the age of 45, people with a disability, ethnic minorities and the unemployed.

The mainspring of the growth in indoor sport was the availability of multi-purpose sports centres of which there were 460 major and 310 smaller in England by 1981. These were essentially local in their impact, and introduced new people to sport without emptying existing facilities or damaging existing clubs. Where they are readily accessible and well marketed and managed, they attract a wide use by the local population.

The targets set in 1983 were based on the development of sports participation and focused on men's and women's participation, better coaching and training and competition venues for international success.

The achievements of the mid 1980s included a significant increase of 150 swimming pools, the establishment of the National Coaching Foundation, and improvements to the Council's National Sports Centres.

Certain negative aspects were recognised in the same report. These were essentially based on inadequate resources, a shortfall in target numbers for women in outdoor sports, too few young people coming into sport, and the continuing need to cater for excellence.

The Sports Council's report Sport in the Community, Into the 90s, A Strategy for Sport 1988-1993[12] summarises the need for sport for all people on both social and economic principles. It also acknowledges that the Sports Council should have an influence in the allocation of resources.

The strategy adopted by the Sports Council for 1988 to 1993 identifies target groups, more facilities and better coordination as priorities for action. Certain target increases in sports participation were ambitious, 1.25 million women and 750,000 men. From an objective point of view it is quite difficult to quantify the function of the Sports Council in achieving these targets, particularly when they have an enabling role. However by introducing a considerable measure of objectivity to their work the Sports Council sought to take stock of their achievements and the improvements in British sport.

Figure 4.1 Participation rates by sex; 1987, 1990.

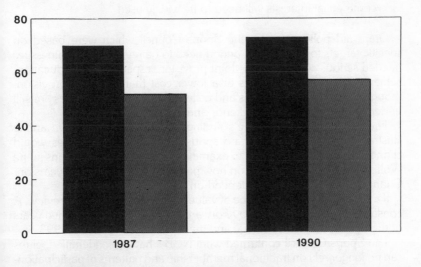

% participating in one activity in last 4 weeks.

■ Men ▨ Women

Moving ahead and planning a strategic response for the 1990s and beyond is the challenge that faces the Sports Council, and all organisations involved with sport and recreation. Just as there was significant change during the early 1980s so the differences between the years 1987-1990 were also important. More people are taking part in sport and recreation than in 1987, 64.5 per cent of the adult population compared to 60.7 per cent in 1987. The increases in participation are significant and the upward trend continues. More women are participating in sport and recreation; over 13 million or 57 per cent of the population. This compares with 15.5 million men or 73 per cent, see figure 4.1. In association with the revised Sports Council will come a strategy to follow those described. The sentiments of the approach to the 1990s is probably determined in the emphasis given in consultation documents. A strategic framework is called for; one which encapsulates a vision of the future whilst having a regard for the good things that have happened.

Sport in the Nineties: new horizons

Demand for sport continues to grow more quickly than current public or private resources can provide for it, so resources will need to be selectively concentrated on promotional programmes for:

- certain target groups and priority or focus sports
- certain geographical areas
- certain types of community facility, both new and adapted
- certain facilities, coaching and administration
- partnership schemes with sporting and other voluntary bodies and commercial interests will need to be widely used

Grant aid policies set by the Sports Council which were based on specific targets for a four year period need to be reviewed. Certain issues needed serious consideration. Joint provision, especially with education, achieves good sports facilities at a lower cost than separate provision, though the majority of schools and colleges with suitable facilities are still under-used, especially at weekends and in the holidays.

The Wolfenden Committee's findings in 1960 certainly gave ample illustration to policy makers and sports organisations that times would change. The reader may wish to examine the summary conclusions in the Wolfenden report and reflect on how pertinent they may be 30 years on. Change is one thing we can depend on.

If a strategy document is to be of value it must receive periodic review. A consultation paper, *Which Way Forward?*[13] considered the first five years of the Sports Council's strategy and made proposals for 1988-1993.

The Sports Council confirmed what NGB's have also identified; clubs can no longer rely on traditional membership and patterns of participation. Some sports are currently suffering a decline in membership while others are enjoying new growth in numbers. The significant increase in the number of sports development officers in recent years has made a tremendous difference to those sports fortunate enough to either have the resources or the grant aid to undertake this important work.

All organisations involved in providing opportunity for sport are beginning to recognise that it would be dangerous to rely on previous numbers of participants and on former levels of grant aid, from whatever source. Local authorities, the Sports Council, and private sponsors have made a significant contribution to voluntary organisations, and governing bodies. The supply of facilities, coaching services, grants for equipment and training, particularly at a local or community level, have been invaluable to clubs. Wherever sports clubs and governing bodies look for money through the 1990s they can expect competition from other bidders. Most grant aiding organisations will therefore expect some kind of return for their money, based on known objectives. Sports development programmes are now an essential part of making progress in UK sport. These plans must also recognise the need for priority areas such as the continued improvement of coach education and training, the requirement to train the volunteers, the improvement of facilities, particularly in the voluntary sector and effective leadership from NGBs and support agencies.

Certainly the Sports Council perceives a different role in the 1990s to that of the early 1980s. Direct involvement is likely to come from:

- supporting the development programmes of national governing bodies, especially those with little or no chance of obtaining major TV fees or corporate sponsorship
- supporting the provision of some facilities for national and international sports training and competition
- helping to develop programmes for training the sports planners and managers of tomorrow
- promoting facility provision for disadvantaged people in our society

Cooperation in planning, managing and evaluating schemes of work will require a fresh challenge for some partners. Managers, be they voluntary or commercial, will benefit from the ability to deliver certain professional skills. Since efficiency and effectiveness are likely to adopt a central position in UK sports organisations, management requires marketing plans, financial preparation and monitoring, and development programmes which consider education and training and operational skills in sport management.

Corporate planning for sport

The Sports Council confirmed priorities and strategies for medium and long term development in 1987. The plan was also seen as a means of persuading the Department of Environment that resources were required to satisfy clearly defined objectives. In identifying priorities, policies and objectives, the Sports Council confirmed its intention to seek value for government money. Competition for government resources requires a business like approach and the Sports Council is now expected, like other quasi-independent organisations, to base its needs on a carefully measured argument.

In defining medium and long term goals the Sports Council was and still is faced with the dilemma of determining a balance between sport participation, and community level involvement or performance and excellence, including the elite and international competition. The issue of urban and rural provision further complicates the exercise, but the need for priorities has to be clearly resolved.

After 20 years of Sports Council contribution to UK sport, a corporate plan will continue to be necessary in order to take a calculated look at specific targets for a defined period. Resource allocation will be dependent upon the defined role and priority given to a task in the plan.

The Minister's review group report on disability[14] provides one example of how management plans can only be as effective as the environment in which they work allows them to be. Disability issues in sport have been understated by many organisations and it is clear from recent research[15] that the Sports Council could spend more of its resources encouraging sport for people with disabilities and that all agencies should consider the disabled when promoting all activities. It would appear from this report that the Sports Council, like all organisations, should regularly redefine priorities and give full regard to changing issues in sport. Evaluation and performance appraisal is therefore a part of the senior management process.

The shift in emphasis towards improved management of resources and programmes is seen in a number of areas. Governing bodies and other national organisations must also prepare development plans at national, regional and, with club support, local levels if they seek to compete for financial support from the grant aiding organisations. For example, money has been allocated to encourage ILAM in the development of education and training in leisure management. This support was offered over a specified period to assist ILAM in achieving agreed targets. The NCF has also been resourced by the Sports Council in order to pursue ambitious plans for coach education and development. In both these examples the Sports Council and government support a commitment to more and better professional and vocational training. The chapter on governing bodies refers to the development of activities which also satisfy Sports Council programmes.

There are further examples of central government and the Sports Council sharing common objectives. The promotion of health, the alleviation of social deprivation, the promotion of international sport, taking a firm position with regard to Britain's role in world sport and the development of excellence are all shared objectives. Each organisation seeks agreement on priorities and on what is meant by satisfying objectives.

British sport, in seeking to develop, looks to the Sports Council for an element of leadership. By providing clearly defined objectives, and incorporating more efficient management practices, they are setting an example to many sports organisations throughout the UK. The Department of National Heritage also needs to justify public expenditure on sport and recreation. This would continue with either party in power.

Regional Councils for Sport and Recreation (RCSR)

Regional identities can be very important in sport and it will continue to be fundamental to the task of identifying need and improving sport and recreation in the UK that the regions of England, Wales, Scotland and Northern Ireland play a part. Currently this role is undertaken by Regional Councils for Sport and Recreation with some variation of policy according to determined priorities. One example of a RCSR, the Northern Council for Sport and Recreation, published a regional sport and recreation strategy in 1982[16] and 1989[17] in which broadly determined aims and objectives were identified. A reviewed strategy with priorities for action and support takes effect in late 1993. In seeking to promote participation and the development of facilities it has been recognised that coordination, consultation and cooperation are essential elements of the strategy. The provision of a regional forum has also enabled local authorities and user groups to appreciate areas of specific interest or sensitivity.

The composition of this regional body has been broad, with major representation coming from local authorities with input from sports bodies (via the Standing Conference of Northern Sport and Recreation), and (according to need) the British Waterways Board, the Countryside Commission, the Forestry Commission, Nature Conservancy Council, the Sports Council, National Parks, Northern Arts, North of England Development Council, Tourist Boards, Trades Union Congress, Water Authorities, the Armed Services, British Sports Association for the Disabled, Higher Education, Departments of the Environment, Education, Agriculture, Fisheries and Food.

Clearly the issues for debate and advice will change, although determining questions for debate will increasingly emerge from a corporate plan and defined objectives. The committees that serve the NCSR, just like the council itself, include representation from local authorities, voluntary and professional bodies, education and various organisations serving sport.

Not only do the committees of the NCSR influence the Sports Council, they can and do act as a focal point for coordinating developments in a region. A development sub-committee and forums, such as the Northern Region Women in Sport, can provide an integrating role through their regular meetings. They can also indicate via a committee if further work or support is required. Better coaching support for women, more effective promotional strategies and childcare services have been highlighted by women. In addition to Women in Sport, groups have been established to consider, Performance and Excellence, Sport for People with Disabilities and Education.

Members of the regional council's committees are also invited to comment upon consultation documents which can include quite specific issues such as the Sports Council's need to use semi-independent agencies who undertake specific specialist functions. This would include such organisations as the National Coaching Foundation. Effective information exchange is also vital if the Sports Council is to remain in touch with the practice of sport. The members of committees, and those they represent, also benefit by receiving details of topical issues including internal reports, forthcoming events, details of grants awarded, information leaflets and future programme of events. This is not an exclusive list of responsibilities or tasks but it does indicate a number of areas of interest.

Summary of key points

1 After 20 years of promoting and enabling sport, the government's advisers on sport policy have been required to undergo a major review. Only time will tell if the reformed Sports Council and the UK Commission will be more successful than the system that has prevailed for so long. One major factor in determining prospects for the future continues to be the provision of adequate resources to effectively promote the desired levels of development in sport.

2 The ability of the Sports Council to execute its duties effectively depends on a number of factors. At a regional and national level there must be an acute regard for the issues that most concern sport. Much of this work is currently achieved through the efforts of its regional officers, although the Regional Councils for Sport and Recreation facilitates this process. Preparing national and regional strategies can provide considerable benefit if those involved appreciate and then address specific problems facing sport.

3 One of the major difficulties experienced by the Sports Council is that they have had to identify priorities based not on whether sporting needs were real or not but on the limited resources at their disposal. Currently those issues causing concern for which there is a lack of money include: a shortage of facilities, including playing fields and the development of performance and excellence. Cut backs in local government facility development brought about by CCT will also influence policies as will central government's interest and encouragement.

4 Whilst the Sports Council's regional network, and the infrastructure of committees and working groups, are an important mechanism in supporting the preparation of regional plans they cannot hope to satisfy all needs. The delivery of sports-related services through partnerships and semi-independent organisations will increase in importance. In seeking to encourage both participation and performance it must be recognised that sport specialists can be of significant benefit. To encourage others, through appropriate grant aid, and to assist in the delivery of organisational objectives, is therefore not a weakness but a strength. When a number of parties

support common ideals and specific targets they are much more likely to succeed by working together.

5 Compulsory competitive tendering, however, will produce the need for a wider network of partnerships. Local authorities will retain their role as client organisations and they will continue to act as contractors in the execution of specific duties. The introduction of competition for local services will undoubtedly increase the contribution of the private sector in sport and recreation management. Regional councils will need to consider an increased role for private organisations in any review of strategy and locally determined objectives. Persuading the private sector to contribute to committees might prove a little more difficult to organise than encouraging the support of local authorities and quasi-organisations. This is not a criticism of any sector, it simply reflects the nature of the competitive environment in which commercial organisations work.

In order to represent the views of sportsmen and sportswomen the Sports Council will need to seek representation from those organisations most involved in the management of sports and recreation. Just as lead bodies for the industry have been established at a national level so regional organisations should include an input from those most involved with the industry whether they be from the public or private sectors (voluntary or commercial).

6 Post CCT promises to bring forward different interests and problems for the Sports Council. Both local government and private sector contractors will need to work to specific targets. It is unlikely that they will seek to develop in areas of either high risk or investment. This suggests that specific groups or targets may be given low priority. The Sports Council has a difficult task in coordinating regional policies particularly when CCT requires the delivery of carefully defined work programmes and strict financial budgets at a local level.

7 It is important that the Sports Council continues to prepare corporate goals and that it exercises its function according to defined objectives. Without adequate resourcing from central government this could become an increasingly difficult task. The current dynamic state of sport and recreation requires that the Sports Council forms the necessary partnerships. Acting as an agent of government they need to encourage and influence partnerships with local authorities and sports organisations who are jointly responsible for budgets that dwarf the annual grant received by the Sports Council. Nevertheless the development of awareness regarding priorities, targeting and management by objectives is a part of the Sports Council's policies and contribution.

8 The Foundation for the Arts, Sportsmatch and the prospects of a large fund from a National lottery suggest a time of promise for many organisations in sport. The Sports Council, with limited funds, will seek to remain an influence in the grant aiding exercise, albeit from a modest base. Whilst one applauds the introduction of new money into sport it is still necessary to ask what criteria are being used to

determine grant allocation and by what measures or mechanisms will schemes be evaluated. The Sports Council may not be the organisation to fulfil all duties but it does seem appropriate that it might have an important role in project monitoring and evaluation. This takes us back to the beginning and the need for a national strategy for sport, one which is properly resourced and effectively managed.

References

1 The Wolfenden Committee on Sport 1960 *Sport and the Community*. HMSO, London.

2 The Sports Council 1972/3 *Provision for Sport* (two reports). The Council, London.

3 The Sports Council 1972 *Sports in the Seventies*. The Council, London.

4 House of Lords Select Committee 1974 *Sport and Recreation*. HMSO, London.

5 White Paper 1975 *Sport and Recreation*. HMSO, Cmnd 6200, London.

6 Department of Education and Science 1991 *Sport and Active Recreation*. HMSO, London.

7 White Paper 1975 *Sport and Recreation*. Cmnd 6200, HMSO, London.

8 Department of Education and Science 1991 *Sport and Action Recreation*. HMSO, London.

9 The Sports Council 1988 *Sport in the Community, Into the 90s, A Strategy for Sport 1988 – 1993*. The Council, London.

10 The Sports Council 1992 *Sport in the Nineties – New Horizons*. The Council, London.

11 The Sports Council 1982 *Sport in the Community: The Next Ten Years*. The Council, London.

12 The Sports Council 1988 *Sport in the Community, Into the 90s, A Strategy for Sport 1988 – 1993*. The Council, London.

13 The Sports Council 1987 *Which Way Forward?* The Council, London.

14 Minister's Review Group 1989 *Building on Ability, Sport for People with Disabilities*. Sport and Recreation Division, (DOE).

15 Sunderland Polytechnic 1988 *Every Body Active Research Papers*. Sports Council (Northern).

16 Northern Council for Sport and Recreation 1982.

17 Northern Council for Sport and Recreation 1989 *A Strategy for Sport and Recreation in the Northern Region, Prospects for the 1990s*.

Further reading

Boothby, Tungatt, Townsend and Collins 1981 Study 22 *A Sporting Chance*. The Sports Council, London.

Fred Coalter with Jonathan Long and Brian Duffield 1986 *Rationale for Public Sector Investment in Leisure*. The Sports Council, London.

Chris Gratton and Peter Taylor 1985 *Sport and Recreation: An Economic Analysis*, Spon.

Chris Gratton and Peter Taylor 1992 *Economics of Leisure Services Management*. Second Edition,Longman/ILAM.

Peter McIntosh and Valerie Charlton 1985 *Study 26: The Impact of Sport for All Policy 1966 – 1984*. The Sports Council, London.

George Torkildsen 1992 Leisure and Recreation Management. Third Edition, Spon/E & F N Spon.

School Sport Forum 1988 *Sport and Young People: Partnership and Action*. The Sports Council, London.

The Sports Council Annual Reports.

The Sports Council 1983 *Structure Function and Aims*.

The Sports Council 1987 *Corporate Plan*.

5 Other bodies involved in sport and physical recreation

Whereas the Sports Council seeks to represent many fundamental issues concerning sport and recreation, there are other public and private sector organisations who concentrate their attention on more specific objectives. This chapter identifies some of those organisations who share an interest in sport and recreation.

The Central Council of Physical Recreation

The CCPR is an independent voluntary body consisting of some 240 governing and representative bodies of sport and physical recreative activities.[1] Its main objects are:

1 To constitute a standing forum where all national governing and representative bodies of sport and physical recreation may be represented and may, collectively or through special groups, where appropriate, formulate and promote measures to improve and develop sport and physical recreation.
2 To support the work of specialist sports bodies and to bring them together with other interested organisations.
3 To act as a consultative body to the Sports Council and other representative or public bodies concerned with sport and physical recreation.

The CCPR has organised a committee structure so that organisations with similar or common interests can meet. These are: Games and Sports Division; Major Spectator Sports Division; Outdoor Pursuits Division; Water Recreation Division; Movement and Dance Division; and Division of Interested Organisations. Essentially the CCPR involves members who have had a long and distinguished career in sport. Many are also involved in sport management, either in a professional or a voluntary capacity.

Governmental involvement in sport through either central government or quasi-government organisations can therefore benefit from the collective wisdom of the CCPR. An independent voice for sport provides a useful and necessary asset for British sport. Indeed a primary role for the CCPR is to represent governing and representative organisations in dealing with organisational liaison.

Services of the CCPR.

Assistance to British sport, and in particular to those involved in managing governing bodies, comes in a variety of forms. A press release service, the encouragement of sponsorship of governing bodies, a communications link with central government and a source of information exchange are all important services offered by the CCPR.

Other issues that receive attention, and which managers may find useful, are:

Publicity for sport sponsorship

Loss of playing fields and sports grounds

Local authorities facilities and charges

Sponsors of sport

Coaching services in sport

Conference for sports administrators

Sport and recreation for the disabled

TV and press and sport and recreation

Parliamentary legislation

Sport and lotteries

Taxation, VAT and corporation tax

Local authority rates

Youth and sport and school sport

International sports contacts

Medical aspects of sport and recreation

With a distinct lack of training for volunteer sports administrators and managers the facility to gain advice on issues like these is invaluable.

Perhaps the one service provided by the CCPR that is best known by the general sporting public is the Community Sports Leaders Award. The CSLA course is now in operation all over the country and is providing volunteer sportsmen and women with basic leadership training. In seeking to recruit many young people and adults, the CCPR has identified a product that is both popular and of benefit to those wishing to become involved in sport. Although the CSLA course can be fairly short, it has succeeded in identifying organisations and practical skills that are of direct benefit. Clearly with some leadership experience and basic training behind them, many people have the opportunity to develop further leadership, coaching or administrative skills.

Since the inception of the CSLA in the early 1980s a Higher Award and a Basic Expedition Award have been added. These courses also fill a gap in the market although the Basic Expedition Award, for example, requires 90 hours of instruction, placing the emphasis on the more committed leader. Work in outdoor recreation requires a particular emphasis on safety, care and preparation. With visits to the countryside becoming more popular this award provides a useful contribution towards encouraging outdoor sports.

Issues facing British sport and the CCPR

One of the fundamental topics that appears to concern British sport is the ability of the CCPR to maintain a strong, independent and representative voice on behalf of the governing bodies. In the preceding section on the background to the CCPR the current position seems to indicate a clearly defined role. However, the CCPR remains rather dependent on the contractual arrangement with the Sports Council for the great majority of its financial requirements. It will be interesting to monitor the CCPR's needs through the 1990s and the extent to which the CCPR relies on Sports Council funding as it continues to develop its leadership function. Nevertheless the Memorandum of Agreement signed by the CCPR and Sports Council officers early in 1988 did resolve one financial debate and it secured a clearer understanding of future roles.

The CCPR remain anxious about a number of management related issues. These include:

1 *The sale and subsequent loss of school playing fields.* Not only are local education authority playing fields at risk, there has also been a similar loss of land owned by other organisations, including local authority departments, private education establishments, voluntary sports clubs and industrial providers. A specific case study is presented in Chapter 8 on issues that arise and further reference is made in the chapter on local government. There is every reason to share the CCPR's anxiety although the power of market forces and the demand for prime development land is a considerable obstacle for sport to overcome. The register of land for sport and recreation should provide the evidence we need for determining future levels of provision.

2 *Competitive tendering, contract management and the effect on public facilities.* There is little doubt that compulsory competitive tendering has been a major issue in sport and recreation. It has affected all organisations involved in the use of publicly owned facilities including sports clubs, governing body elite squads and the recreational user. Chapter 3, on local government, makes specific reference to the implications of compulsory competitive tendering. The nature of the facility management and the determination to satisfy financial objectives, will undoubtedly change the emphasis in sports provision and management through the 1990s. The scenario will apply irrespective of whether local authorities or the private sector are managing contracts and facilities. It is difficult to envisage a situation where a contractor will be prepared to sacrifice economic targets for locally determined sporting or social criteria which were

not identified in the contract and for which no provision has been made.

3 *The National Non Domestic Rate.* The imposition of a business rate in the form of the National Non Domestic Rate (NNDR) has an impact on the financial viability of voluntary sports organisations. Local authorities do have power, however, to award up to 100 per cent discretionary rate relief, with 75 per cent of the relief funded through central government. Sports clubs must be organised and prepared to present an effective lobby if this opportunity is to be taken up. For many smaller organisations the payment of rates is one of the most significant items in their annual expenditure. Chapter 3 also considers this item in the financing of local government.

4 *The taxation of national governing bodies of sport.* The need to pay Corporation Tax, and Capital Gains Tax where appropriate, is a burden on those organisations in sport and recreation who merely seek to develop and invest in their organisation and in sport provision. Although the payment of tax may be more acutely felt by some national governing bodies it is also a pertinent issue for many smaller clubs. Without a significant political commitment by central government to assist sport and recreation in the United Kingdom the voluntary sector will continue to find investment, in facilities and programmes, difficult.

5 *The development of a coherent role for sports sponsorship.* The availability of sports sponsorship currently represents a major factor for many events and development programmes. Sports participation at all levels, and in many sports, is partly dependent on attracting private sector money. Therefore it is important that sponsors' money should be used for the benefit of all sport and that companies are encouraged by government to invest in small as well as large organisations and events. The introduction of Sportsmatch in late 1992, with 3 million of matching funding for new sponsorship is an exciting opportunity for those who have the ability to attract sponsorship at a local level.

6 *The availability of central government funds.* Throughout this text reference is made to the role of central government in encouraging or developing sport and recreation. The lack of a clearly identified plan and limited resources invested are a constraint on growth. Changes in education and facility management, discussed in Chapter 3, highlight the need to consider a national strategy for sport and recreation which is adequately funded and supported by central government.

7 *The structure of sport within the UK.* In order to survive, sport and recreation organisations need to be well managed with an infrastructure at regional and national level that provides appropriate support. As demands on sports administrators grow so professional assistance, including training programmes and technical support packages, become a necessity. With constraints on how much administration the voluntary sector can handle, governing bodies

must address this issue. In order that UK sports can consider growth there is a further need to provide and develop a strong and coherent structure for sports administration. The chapters dealing with the Sports Council, governing bodies and other organisations explore this matter further.

Resource management in British sport is clearly going to make a significant impact over the next few years. For reasons outlined above, there remains a need for one organisation to protect and promote, without undue interference. The role of that organisation however must be clearly defined.

With so much depending on the voluntary sector, British sport currently lacks firm and clear direction and a positive political commitment by central government. It will be of vital importance to the sportsman and woman that their interests are acted upon where appropriate. Rhetoric will be of scant comfort if necessary resources are not provided.

It is essential to British sport that the voluntary sector prospers. Government could and should play a significant enabling role in this. Every governing body of sport and sports club will also need to consider the benefits of an effectively prepared and implemented business or development plan. The greatest qualities of British sport must be protected and their potential developed. This can only be achieved if the parent organisations are both recognised and involved. Chapter 6 includes case material that suggests this process is at least underway.

Essentially coordination, cooperation and collaboration will each become very important, both in British and international sport. Salaried and non salaried managers primarily from the voluntary sector will increasingly benefit from a shared approach to problem solving. Managers involved in British sport cannot be expected to have an insight into every organisation, or a solution to all problems. The CCPR therefore provides a useful supportive organisation for those involved in British sport to receive information, exchange views, and encourage basic leadership training.

There are also some fundamental problems facing British sport which require considered professional judgement. A number of specific issues have been identified although the situation underlying most of these issues is the same. The voluntary sector in particular will become increasingly dependent on the generation of its own resources. These will primarily be financial but the development of human potential, including leaders, coaches, and administrators, will also be important.

National Coaching Foundation

The National Coaching Foundation (NCF) was formed in 1983 with the support of the Sports Council, the Central Council of Physical Recreation (CCPR), the British Association of National Coaches (BANC), the Department of Education and Science (DES), the British Olympic Association (BOA), the British Association of Sports Science (BASS), the British Association of Sport and Medicine (BASM) and Institutes of Higher

Education in England, Wales, Scotland and Northern Ireland. The major organisations continue to be represented on the NCF Board of Directors.

In 1987 the National Coaching Foundation was designated as the coaching arm of the Sports Council, responsible for the coordination of coaching and coach education. Working on a UK basis, and in partnership with the four national sports councils, the NCF is required to formulate policy and coordinate the implementation of the recommendations from 'Coaching matters'. Working with major partners such as local authorities, national governing bodies of sport and further and higher education and associated with networks in physical education, sports science and sports medicine, the NCF delivers various programmes of work.

The NCF does seek to encourage partnerships with representative organisations but it has a specific obligation towards service delivery and in particular coaches and coaching.

It is widely recognised that British sport lacks adequate resources. Although finance is clearly a major issue the primary impetus behind sports development is the quality of people involved. Managers and volunteers, part time and full time, who put effort into our sporting culture remain a most important asset. Those who are involved in the promotion of participation will recognise that the skills of leadership, coaching and managing are vital.

Since 1983 the NCF has developed a range of services and products designed to provide a service to coaches. The range of products and services used varies from training programmes for novice coaches to master coaches across the whole of the UK and overseas, to the development of research and information services. Much of the actual presentation of courses, seminars and conferences for coaches has been organised through a National Network of Coaching Centres. The Coaching Centres have also contributed to the development of support services to coaches in their region.

The NCF, funded originally from the Sports Council, has become a recognised organisation working towards the improvement of coaching in England, Wales, Scotland and Northern Ireland. In the Sports Council's strategy document published in 1988 it commented that:

> The Council regards the setting up of The National Coaching Foundation and its associated network of National Coaching Centres throughout the UK as one of the major successes of the past five years.[2] It is an initiative which has attracted widespread support from many quarters, both home and abroad.

The NCF needs to generate a proportion of its total expenditure and to achieve this objective it has established a company limited by guarantee with charitable status to undertake its principal objectives. A subsidiary trading company, Coachwise, earns profits on NCF products and services, then covenants funds to the NCF charity. The services offered include information and advice on coach development programmes with courses run for all levels of coaching expertise. These are administered both from the head office in Leeds and the regional coaching centres. In order that service delivery can be at a level, and in a location, that best satisfies the coaches a system of registered institutions across the United Kingdom offers further support to assist in this process.

It is estimated that over 400,000 people work in sport as coaches, officials or professionals and it is to them that the NCF directs its services. With a vibrant support network to our six million sportsmen and women the quality of sport, at all levels, will undoubtedly improve.

Comment has been made elsewhere that the development of British sport will increasingly depend on partnerships. The ability and willingness of sports organisations to recognise needs and share expertise is vital to ensure future success. With continued support from government, agencies such as the NCF will play an important role in effecting these partnerships. Local authorities, governing bodies and individual coaches will also need to recognise, perhaps even more fully than at present, the benefits of cooperation.

The involvement of the NCF in the development of national policy groups in Scottish/National Vocational Qualifications, youth sport, education and training, sports administration, sports leadership, sports science, information services and prison services confirms the importance of the role that the NCF has developed since 1983.[3] The Sports Council's review of coaching and the publication of Coaching Matters made a number of recommendations for implementation[4]. One of the most significant is the merger of BISC (the British Association of Sports Coaches) and the NCF under one umbrella organisation providing for coaching and coach education in the UK.

The services offered are aimed at individual coaches' needs and fundamentally provide access to opportunities for continuing development. The NCF seeks to contribute at a time when profiles of sports are set to change. During the 1990s more people will participate in sport, the demand for excellence will increase and improving standards of provision will be expected.

Local authorities, governing bodies, sports clubs and committed coaches alike should have prepared a development strategy. There are many levels at which this would then function; coaching is only one dimension.

1 All organisations in sport and recreation should consider the merits of a development strategy which incorporates coach development. The strategy should also recognise the potential of working in partnership with other organisations.

2 Individual elements should be detailed over a three or five year period to encourage progress and review.

3 In the case of coach development the NCF is a service organisation. It requires others, acting alone or in partnership, to consider and accept an awareness of needs.

4 A profile of coach development is important within our governing bodies and sports clubs. Coaches at all levels should receive encouragement to pursue training programmes.

Good coaching must be one of the most cost effective ways of developing sports participation and excellence. The contribution of the NCF needs to be assessed in the light of the effort that others make in pursuing beneficial goals. Although some governing bodies and local authorities have carefully considered the future, there are many gaps in provision. The encouraging signs are that the Sports Council and the NCF are actively promoting a progressive approach to sports development through the implementation of their own plans.

Within the next few years the UK Sports Commission (UKSC) and the English Sports Council will have established policies and programmes and in so doing will have the NCF available to coordinate coaching and coach education throughout the UK. Further opportunities exist for cooperation and development including the establishment of an NCF membership division, a National Coaches Association, which would embrace the membership of BISC. The foundation of a National Sports Science Institute would also assist the development of performance and excellence. The benefits of even closer working links with the Sport and Recreation Training Consortium and the National Sports Medicine Institute might include the preparation of new materials and the coordination of services to the benefit of those involved with sports performance.

At a local and regional level the NCF seeks to develop and deliver coach education programmes through a network of franchised centres. This will ultimately require teams of specialists within the NCF working with various partner agencies to develop, coordinate and implement new programmes. The development of programmes through higher education might also include courses and qualifications at first and second degree levels. Indeed, a European consortium of institutions in higher education is already preparing a masters degree in sport coaching.

There remain exciting opportunities for the development of coaches and coach education in the UK and it is apparent that the NCF is well positioned to take advantage of the developments in S/NVQs, Champion Coaching and the Education and Training Consortium for Sport and Recreation as well as building on the strengths established over the last ten years or so.

Institute of Leisure and Amenity Management (ILAM)

Just as the CCPR is a representative organisation actively encouraging leadership the NCF also works collaboratively pursuing the development of coaching. Moving to the level of leisure management, the needs of professionals are represented by the Institute of Leisure and Amenity Management (ILAM), and the Institute of Baths and Recreation Management (IBRM). A profile of ILAM, will serve to represent some of the issues currently facing those in sport and recreation management.

The Institute was formed on January 1st 1983, following the amalgamation of the former Institute of Park and Recreation

Administration (IPRA), the Institute of Municipal Entertainment (IME), the Institute of Recreation Management (IRM) and the Association of Recreation Managers (ARM).

ILAM is an independent company limited by guarantee, financially supported by annual subscriptions, various promotional ventures, conferences and seminars. Membership of the Institute is approaching 7,000 and is drawn from the public and private sectors. The various disciplines are also represented in the membership, which ensures the ability to respond to a broad and dynamic industry.

The principal objectives of the Institute are:

- to act as an effective lobby whenever proposed legislation is likely to
  effect the industry
- to recognise the education and training needs of the leisure industry
- to promote the delivery of effective education and training programmes
- to provide a recognised professional qualification based on demonstrated competence
- to offer advisory services in careers and technical matters
- to encourage the professional development of the Institute's membership
- to cooperate with all appropriate organisations concerned with the leisure industries[5]

Clearly ILAM, in representing leisure management has a broader remit than just sport and physical recreation. ILAM, managed by an elected Council, is serviced by a sub-committee structure made up of members. Day to day operation of ILAM's business is managed by a Director, and professional and administrative staff, based at the Institute's headquarters in Lower Basildon.

Conferences, seminars and a training programme of short courses are organised centrally, operating at a national and regional level, for the benefit of the industry. Access is not restricted to members of the Institute since it has the declared goal of catering to the needs of the leisure profession.

Regional conferences and seminars also take place, although these are organised through the elected executive committees for each of the regions. The map of ILAM's regional structure illustrates one approach to the satisfaction of individual members' needs. This encourages local debate on national issues, the delivery of local training opportunities, and the facility to discuss the institute's policies which are of wide interest.

The Institute offers an examination package to members but it encourages others to provide the education and training. Exemptions from individual units of the examination programme are possible for those academic institutions offering appropriate programmes. In common with education trends nationally and internationally, courses are geared towards a modular and credit accumulation and transfer structure.

The *Leisure Manager* magazine provides a monthly review of leisure related subjects. It is free to members and is available on subscription to those who are not. A weekly direct mail service provides a regular update on appointment opportunities and provides for communication between members.

The need to plan ahead has been identified by ILAM. After five years of consolidation and growth, the Institute has sought to determine its five year development[6]. With the pace of change in the leisure sector likely to accelerate during the 1990s, it is vital to the interests of the profession that the Institute is organised, able to respond and sufficiently flexible. There is no example more pertinent at this time than the redefinition of public and private sector roles in delivering leisure opportunities. Fundamental changes will take place to the character and the performance of leisure facilities. Essentially the Institute recognises that it has a responsibility, to its members and to the industry, to cast an influence on the market place.

Other issues will continue to effect the success of ILAM. They include:

- its ability to broaden the membership base, particularly into the private sector, and to the industry generally
- the effectiveness of regional programmes designed to cater for individuals operating under greater pressure. Programmes will need to be relevant and viable and regional support systems will be required to deliver these packages
- the opportunity for members to access information and support services on technical, educational or career related matters
- the development of effective education and training programmes through institutions of further and higher education. The Institute's own examination system will complement the delivery of exempted courses throughout the UK
- the ability to encourage and attract sponsorship of selected professional initiatives

The relevance of most professional bodies to the young practitioner is that they provide an opportunity, away from the formal work environment, to meet, to read or to have contact with professional peers and to share experiences. There are a number of ways in which this may occur, through publications, seminar debate, conferences or simply correspondence.

Over recent years the development of ILAM's professional examination structure has been modified to encourage membership. ILAM has further promoted this process by encouraging colleges and universities to validate their own leisure management programmes. Subject to appropriate validation the Institute will grant exemption from selected professional body examinations.

If the leisure industry has previously lacked a professional lobby it is clear that circumstances have now changed. With the industry set for a dynamic decade, it will be essential for organisations like ILAM to provide an effective lobby. Compulsory competitive tendering, contract management, quality management systems, unitary authorities, the effects of privatisation of water and the forces working towards economic measures of performance rather require dynamic professional leadership both regionally and nationally.

The Institute of Leisure and Amenity Management has been successful, since its formation in 1983, in presenting a relatively coordinated approach towards the leisure profession. Much has been done to encourage education and training both nationally and regionally, with officers of the institute being proactive at both levels. The recent and extensive development of sport, recreation and leisure courses in higher education provides an appropriate example of the need for a professional institute offering advice whenever pertinent. Compulsory competitive tendering and contract management has also placed a keen emphasis on management priorities and skills in delivering client and contractor responsibilities. ILAM has offered assistance to the profession in this direction by supporting the publication of some comprehensive management manuals.

ILAM's role appears particularly important at present. It is vital that the institute presents a strong and representative face to government and to those in a position to influence the leisure industry. One strength here must be the major influence that practicing managers have on the determination of the institute's policies and management.

Leisure provision has taken on an international dimension with multinational organisations diversifying into leisure development and management. Apart from developing specific links with individual organisations ILAM has also established and promoted international partnerships, inside Europe and beyond, which enhance the status of an increasingly significant service industry.

Perhaps the most important issue of all, for ILAM and for the Institute of Baths and Recreation Management (IBRM), is confirmation of a professional identity acknowledged and respected for the contribution it makes. The focus of attention on customers and the quality of service provision rather presumes that ILAM and similar organisations, like IBRM, might seek a coordinated approach to professional development. The leisure industry is undergoing such dramatic change that it requires integrated policies and priorities.

Sports Aid Foundation (SAF)

In considering the needs of leaders, coaches, and managers the focus of attention is on the delivery of a service. The encouragement of sport and recreation also involves participants of varying ages and abilities. National governing bodies have a clearly defined obligation to one sport but there are other organisations which have a wider focus. Two contrasting organisations which illustrate this diversity are the Sports Aid Foundation (SAF) and the British Sports Association for the Disabled (BSAD). The issues that they provoke are different because they have distinct objectives. Managers should appreciate that different groups have different needs, and the selection of SAF and BSAD, as examples, will illustrate some of these differences.

Recognised by the Sports Council, the CCPR and the British Olympic Association (BOA) the SAF became effective in 1976. The SAF is an entirely independent organisation managed by a Board of Governors who, as volunteers, award Elite and International grants to amateurs for legitimate out of pocket expenses which were incurred in preparation and training.[7] The appropriate governing body is required to provide its consent.

Elite grants go to those who have Olympic or world medal potential. International grants are awarded to competitors of proven ability who are expected to compete with distinction in the Olympic Games. Development grants are used to encourage young athletes who demonstrate potential for excellence, and athletes with a disability are offered grants amounting to ten per cent of the money available to able-bodied athletes. All amateur sports are considered although team sports need to submit individual applications.

Regional companies have been established to assist sportsmen and sportswomen who do not qualify for either the Elite or the International grants. In order that the regional company may consider a grant, the request must be channelled through the appropriate liaison officer of the sport concerned. Essentially these grants are for assistance with travel, equipment, preparation, coaching and training expenses.

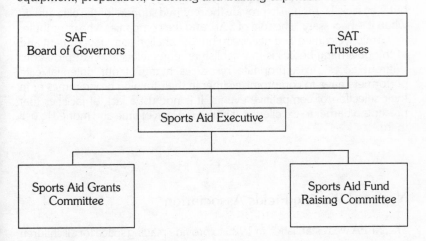

Figure 5.1 Sports Aid organisation

The SAF and SAT are legally separate bodies. SAF Ltd raises funds to help talented sportspeople while SAT is a charity to help young people develop their sporting talents.

Support for Sports Aid has come from a variety of sources. The 1991-1992 report comments on the largest award of 314,000 coming from the Foundation for Sport and the Arts. This money was targeted for the 1992

Olympic Games, with the express purpose of offering training grants to athletes in the British team who were not eligible for Minet Awards. The Minet Insurance's sponsorship of Awards for Olympic Excellence continued but as an additional resource to those raised by the SAF. The Sports Aid Enterprises lottery, SAF's fully owned lottery company, also provided 503,000 in 1992. A variety of initiatives and fund raising events take place each year across the country to raise additional moneys. In the same year over 750,000 was awarded in Elite, International and Minet Awards, more than double the previous year's amount. The Sports Aid Foundation Charitable Trust has also recently achieved the ambition of creating a 1 million reserve which will guarantee future support to British sportsmen and women. Indeed in 1992 2,649 sportspeople received grants from the Sports Aid Foundation, including regional and associated companies and the SAF Charitable Trust, amounting to nearly 1.25 million.

Whilst it would be understandable for sports-minded people to reflect on the appropriateness of a government grant for our Olympic sportspeople, it remains a credit to so many people that Sports Aid makes such a significant contribution.

It may seem a sad irony that British sport demands its champions yet so much responsibility for resourcing training and competition falls on the individuals themselves or the private sector. Leisure managers in the public and voluntary sectors actively encourage the pursuit of excellence but they lack the money to provide the required support for the elite athlete when it is necessary. The role of SAF, and the companies who contribute, is warmly welcomed and necessary but the challenge to government and to the governing bodies is to establish an equitable system of provision. Without access to appropriate resources many of our potential elite performers have to compromise either in their training programmes or in their selection of competitive events. It is not just a lack of facilities that presents a barrier to excellence, it is also the lack of time and money to use them.

National Playing Fields Association

The NPFA was established in 1925 to provide playing space for all children and young people, and to encourage the physical and social skills vital to their development.

Since that time NPFA research identified a minimum target for outdoor playing space. In 1986 the NPFA reconsidered its own target, set in 1938, for a minimum of six acres (2.43 ha), per 1000 population of outdoor playing space[8]. This target, for the guidance of local authorities and others, was reaffirmed in 1986.8 Assessing actual pitch requirements was, however, referred to the Sports Council's guide-lines.

Loss of playing fields

With only finite space available for industrial, commercial and domestic housing developments, great pressure is currently being placed on land allocation. Public and private sectors alike have, in recent years, been involved in numerous cases of either recreational land loss or planning appeals in defence of playing fields. The undoubted loss of playing fields in the UK during the 1980s has been of great concern to the NPFA, the CCPR, and the Sports Council. It has proved difficult, however, under prevailing political and economic circumstances either to quantify the loss in precise terms, or to bring sufficient influence to bear on policy makers. NPFA resources do not enable them to purchase, or assist in the purchase, of more land than they do already.

A register of land used for recreational purposes is at last being prepared following a recognition by government of the potential problem. The research is being coordinated by the Sports Council. Indeed it was only in fairly recent history that local authorities were invited by central government to declare any appropriate education land as surplus to requirements. Falling school roles and schools faced with closure suggested that less land may be required. The context of the argument however, or so it seems, is not one based on recreational need but on investment appraisal by ambitious land owners. Where it has proved attractive to attempt to sell for alternative use, the land owner could stand to pocket a heavily weighted financial return. Loss of recreation space, which is afterall irrecoverable, remains the NPFA's most worrying problem.

The NPFA, unlike the CCPR, is in a position to offer some grant aid assistance to protect or improve playing field provision. It is left to the Sports Council to consider grant aiding an organisation wishing to purchase sports fields. The application for grant aid would normally have to accord with identified priorities in a region. Clearly any land made available for industrial or domestic housing development is much more valuable than existing playing field use. Sports organisations stand little chance therefore of making realistic bids for purchase.

The National Playing Fields Association has proposed a ten point plan to fight the threat to playing fields, in which it urges the public to carefully monitor all local sources of information including Council minutes and newspaper articles.

Meetings should be called which involve a wide cross section of local sports organisations, politicians and representatives from interested bodies. In addition to keeping NPFA informed, every effort must be made to check any plans for the disposal of recreational land against the structure plan which each district will have produced. When faced with an application for planning, particularly where there may be a threat to local playing fields, the NPFA advises any interested party to check the availability of playing field space against its national targets of six acres of playing field space per 1000 of population. The case study in Chapter 8 provides an illustration of one organisation's fight to protect playing fields from the developers. There can be little doubt that it is imperative that threatened organisations should carefully prepare and practise their defence. Such a line of action is likely to involve meetings with the local authority, correspondence with the Member of Parliament for the area and discussions with the local media. No form of action, even letters to the Secretary of State at the Department of National Heritage, the Department for Education and the Department for the Environment, should be overlooked.

Those under threat will need to fight a carefully organised battle, using organisations like the NPFA for valuable support whenever appropriate.

Local authorities and voluntary organisations are encouraged to utilise the NPFA's advice and to contact them direct for specific guidance. In Chapter 9 a realistic case study illustrates both the character and the complexity of this issue. Certainly anyone interested in the development of sport and recreation might well want to know what a local authority has adopted as its own standard of provision. This standard can then be measured against both the NPFAs target and the Sports Council recommendations.

Clearly the NPFA has wider interests. Children's play areas and kick-about facilities are also regarded as important. Consideration of safety factors, training provision and a publications list are further dimensions to the NPFA's work.

Apart from any future consideration of low cost durable and rugged adventure playgrounds, the overriding issue remains adequate provision of facilities. To this end providers in general, and voluntary organisations in particular, will also need to consider different market segments when considering the enhancement of facilities. The need for facilities will feature more strongly as demand continues to increase for sport, recreation and play areas. Parents and adults will not only need to be seen as providing encouragement to children, they will also be required to take a great interest in, and responsibility for, the development of their children.

Sport for people with a disability

According to the Office of Population Census Survey (OPCS) in 1988 there are approximately 6.2 million adults with disability in Britain. It is important, therefore, to direct the attention of policy makers, fund providers and enablers to the needs of a significant group of people.

Although 69 per cent of people with a disability are elderly there are also many such people who do not wish to be defined as such whatever their age. We must also recognise that there are many children with a disability who fall outside official statistics but who may benefit from opportunities in sport and recreation.

For the purposes of this section people with a disability include those with learning difficulties and those with physical and sensory disabilities. Sporting opportunities for people in the following categories of disability:

spinal cord, visual, hearing, cerebral palsy, amputee, learning difficulties and *les autres* are promoted by seven National Disability Sports Organisations as well as the British Sports Association for the Disabled (BSAD) which is a multi disability organisation. Although each national organisation has its own constitution, a distinct identity and a purpose, cooperation and coordination does takes place.

Sports provision for people with a disability is going through a period of transition. The delegation, or acceptance, of responsibility for providing sport for the disabled is now a major issue. Creating an awareness of disability and persuading essential resources from public and private sectors has not been easy but must continue. A case study at the end of this section presents an argument for greater coordination between disability organisations in creating a unified voice for policy and financial support and changes in regional and local sporting infrastructure.

Whilst it may be possible to beat the drum and argue that more should be done, a positive message must also be reported. There are pockets of excellence activity across Great Britain. Disabled sportsmen and women are achieving standards of excellence; facility provision has been improved and there are signs of an increase in levels of general awareness. At the same time it should be recognised that current attention on sport should be on the ability of the individual and not the disability. Such an attitude would lend itself to a more meaningful consideration of mainstream sport and integration into mainstream activities. Provision should be made in sport for everyone, and it should not exclude one section of our community. At the same time it is widely recognised that people with a disability may choose to participate in a separate club or in exclusive events.

The Paralympics, which only started in Rome in 1960, has provided a number of outstanding sportsmen and women with appropriate recognition. The strength and performance of the British team in the Paralympics in Seoul, 1988, and again in Barcelona in 1992 was particularly encouraging due to some good television coverage. In reaching for excellence it is important to establish a wide base of participation.

The concept of sport for all... relates to policies which seek to extend the benefits of sport to as many people as possible.
    It is comprehensive ... embracing sport in many different forms, from recreational physical activity to high level competition.
(European Sport For All Charter)

However sport for all is not yet a reality. People with a disability do not enjoy sufficient levels of opportunity or access to sport. Although 30 per cent of the population in Europe participates in sport on a regular basis, only three per cent of those with a disability participate in sports organisations for the disabled.

People with a disability require recognition and support from the public sector in terms of policy formulation, facility provision and adequate resourcing.

Emphasis has been placed in recent years on the importance of adequate facility provision, particularly access and egress. A Sports Council (1982) publication, *Sports Centres for Disabled People*,[9] provided evidence of an encouraging growth of opportunity expressed in terms of the number of sports centres, access arrangements, centre facilities and general information of use to those with special needs.

Simply providing well designed sports facilities for people with disabilities will never be enough. Improving the opportunity to participate in sport depends on a number of other factors. It is necessary, therefore, to highlight the need for demonstrated good practice based on well formed policies. Qualified and experienced leaders, coaches and managers need to confirm an appreciation of needs for the disabled.

British Sports Association for the Disabled (BSAD)[10]

The BSAD assumed a formal identity in 1961 following the significant contribution made by Sir Ludwig Guttman in bringing together sports organisations seeking to serve people with a disability.

Subsequent programmes of activity led to the introduction and development of specific competitions for people with a disability nationally and regionally, including Wales, Scotland, and Northern Ireland. In July 1987 the BSAD coordinated with seven major National Disability Sports Organisations (NDSOs), with 33 national members. Participation in the Association's activities involved 560 sports clubs and 55,000 people with a disability.

The BSAD is amongst the best known organisations involved with sport for the disabled. Regional associations and officers of the BSAD are active in encouraging local authorities and agencies but they have more recently become proactive in identifying needs and offering services.

The objectives of the BSAD stress such key words as encouraging, promoting, coordinating, coaching and training, and liaising. Essentially these characteristics underline the enabling role.

The BSAD will continue to develop its relationship with National Governing Bodies, the Sports Council, the CCPR, the British Olympic Association, the National Coaching Foundation and many others. Indeed, cooperation and coordination is increasingly important to all sports organisations in seeking to satisfy their ambitions and in securing required funding from whatever source.

Sport and disability: management issues

1 A prime objective in developing sport in the community must be to encourage clubs to include greater numbers of people with disabilities in their membership. Most sports clubs are found in the voluntary sector and as such provide a valuable resource. Individuals

and groups, both able-bodied and disabled, would also benefit from policies that supported and developed integrated programmes.

2 The British Sports Association for the Disabled, in a survey of provision and need, recognised the importance of National Governing Bodies (NGBs) as the mainstream provider. Indeed, coaching and training should remain with the remit of the NGBs both for those who coach people with a disability and those who are themselves disabled. It is disappointing, therefore, to note that 77 per cent of NGBs made no mention of the disabled in their New Approach submissions to the Sports Council. British sports associations need to profess their commitment to sport for all and to sport equity. A concern towards the encouragement and development of integration whenever it is both appropriate and suited to the needs of an individual should also be recognised by all organisations in sport.

3 Local authorities are assumed to be the recognised providers of resources and opportunities for all people. Unfortunately, it has been difficult for the BSAD to quantify the nature of local authority services for people with a disability. As the Greater London Association for the Disabled (GLAD) Report (1987)[11] confirms, there are too few policy statements on the needs of people with a disability. The Every Body Active demonstration project, supported by the Sports Council, and based in the North East of England also confirmed that minimal policy and sports development provision had been incorporated into the English local authorities competitive tendering documentation.[12] The conclusion offered by the BSAD suggests the need to develop partnerships between NGBs, the Sports Council and any new parent organisations. Any promotion of nationally validated sports programmes must come, clearly, through the NGBs. By their very nature, governing bodies at national and regional levels rely on a significant contribution from the voluntary sector and as such might feel that collaboration with others is essential.

4 The National Coaching Foundation (NCF) in conjunction with the NGBs, BSAD and the local authorities should work together on a programme of 'disability awareness'.[11] The Scottish Sports Association for the Disabled (SSAD), for example, has held a fourteen event programme of national and international sports which, although marked by a lack of media interest, provided the NGBs with an opportunity to respond to the call for support. Whilst there is no doubt that participation by individuals with disabilities has increased over the last ten years, the critical area of need is for trained leaders and coaches to develop participation. It is important for coaches to operate locally and, wherever possible, with integrated clubs in order that the gap between high level performance and grass-roots participation can be reduced.

5 The NGBs might turn their attention to the human resources currently available as leaders and consider how they might be

developed into trained coaches. At the moment too few NGBs provide basic coaching courses which are designed to cater for the needs of all athletes.

6 The Scottish Sports Association for the Disabled suggests an attack on four fronts including: cooperation between NGBs and SSAD to look at award schemes; NGBs of non-risk sports to develop coach education programmes for those involved in a number of sports; the need to consider a national strategy for coach education; and to encourage greater coach involvement. Coaches can adapt to working with people with a disability more easily than can those who lack a sporting background develop coaching skills.

Of some concern, however, must be the gap between the Sports Council's policies and work that is actually going on at the local level. A proactive approach is required since it is not good enough to rely on disability organisations which merely react to problems as they are experienced. This can be accomplished with regional and local structures working in a coordinated fashion.

There is a need for a policy commitment which is designed to increase opportunities for people with a disability. Such a policy commitment is required of the regional councils for sport and recreation and the local authority councils in their area.

Detailed action plans are required which necessitate the delegation of responsibility to a senior officer in a Leisure Services Department. Such an officer would be required to develop opportunities, establish 'mechanisms for coordination', liaise with outside parties and consider other special groups. Within the action plan an officer of the regional council would be charged with the responsibility for developing 'a programme of support work' by statutory and voluntary organisations, including funding. The BSAD and the United Kingdom Sports Association for People with Mental Handicap (UKSAPMH) would need to review structures for working at local level and work priorities.

Local authorities should identify people with disabilities, appreciate their needs, disseminate information, improve access, review transport provision, offer price concessions and develop the work of community sport teams.

The second point to make is that, whilst competitive sport has been a focus of attention, it involves a minority of disabled individuals. Development work at a local level must be emphasised to local councils and to regional offices of NGBs. A regional and local structure is necessary but it is likely that this can only be achieved gradually. Certain services can be presented fairly easily and perhaps must be seen as a priority. Training for leaders and coaches in disability awareness is required so that they might be able to develop programmes more effectively. It must be one goal to integrate people with disabilities who are interested in sport with mainstream clubs and competitions. For this reason a wide range of organisations must be consulted. In particular the youth service and the health authority should be included in all liaison and communication between organisations. It is vital that all who may be concerned with the provision of opportunity should be aware of sources of advice, help and money.

On a number of occasions the need for collaboration and cooperation between organisations has been expressed. This section has attempted a consideration of sport and disability with organisations, both specific and non- specific, who may be able to contribute. The BSAD is certainly important in this but, as is now recognised, they cannot do everything for all people interested in sport and disability[13]. Local authorities and voluntary organisations must take a positive role. Together with continued government interest in disability, and a commitment by the Sports Council through the 1990s, the current situation should improve considerably.

Case Study:
Federation of Disability Sports Organisations Yorkshire and Humberside

Introduction
The following case study is set in Yorkshire and Humberside and highlights benefits of cooperation and coordination that could become valuable across the country. The regional strategy subject report on sport for people with disabilities addresses fundamental needs which are covered elsewhere in this chapter.[14] Moreover the recommendations of the regional strategy recognise that policy commitments should be made by local authorities and other organisations. Priorities are consequently identified for training, access, participation, resources, communication and liaison, promotion and publicity and future action, (including an action plan which focuses on the implementation of the strategy).

Organisations involved
The principal organisations involved, British Blind Sports, British Deaf Sports Council, British Sports Association for the Disabled and Disport (representing people with learning disabilities in the region) have decided to work together and from a position of equal equity to seek the full involvement of people with a disability in all aspects of sport and recreation in Yorkshire and Humberside. The objectives of the Federation focus on cooperation, development, resources, training, monitoring and evaluation. In order to achieve documented objectives a political and staffing structure has to be put in place.

Federation objectives
Under Phase One of a three year scheme, commencing in April 1993 and supported by the regional Sports Council and West Yorkshire Grants, staff appointments in the form of a coordinator, four regional resource officers and three clerical positions undertook duties that previously would have been shared in an uncoordinated fashion across a number of disability organisations. The Sports Council for Yorkshire and Humberside has committed £150,000 over the years 1993-1996 to support the federation with every prospect of similar funding from West Yorkshire Grants. Each of the four disability organisations has also maintained its separate regional identity and constitution with the Federation, acting as a vehicle for securing added value for the partnership. A memorandum of understanding has been agreed between each of the four partner organisations who already enjoy charitable status. Common areas of work, for example children in sport, have become a key area for the Federation. The Federation will work with schools, including special schools, in providing awareness training and support mechanisms. There had previously been a lack of student records profiling the

sporting achievements of children with a disability and a lack of teacher awareness and skills working in a mainstream situation. The need to attract sponsorship from commercial organisations and companies for a variety of activities is also something better sought in combined effort rather than in competition. Indeed, continued funding after the three year period of grant aid will become a major test for the Federation.

Initially the regional resource officers have an important research role in identifying individuals with disabilities and appreciating their local needs. This will involve cooperation beyond the Federation to include social services, education authorities, schools, local sports clubs, youth officers and teachers. The coordinator has tasks associated with fund raising, maintaining effective communications with disability organisations and administering the project. This position is also responsible for influencing the policy makers within local government, regional and national governing bodies of sport and the disability organisations themselves. It is a political role which will promote the long-term viability of the project and greatly assist in achieving the Federation's objectives. An audit of current levels of provision in sports facilities, the preparation of policy statements are important outcomes to the work of a Federation of Disability Sports Organisations.

The management committee is made up of two representatives from each of the four disability organisations and the coordinator, plus a single representative of West Yorkshire Grants and the regional Sports Council who are on the committee as observers.

Continued opportunities

With many local authorities and national governing bodies employing sports development officers at a regional and local level and with an increasing number of officers with a responsibility for special needs, the Federation can play a key role in identifying needs, supporting key agencies and maintaining an important training and awareness input. Sport development forums focusing on community needs should also provide a useful means of integrating the work, experience and ideas of a number of individuals. It is an important advantage of the Federation that it is working from the previous experience of four disability organisations and that support and communication networks already exist for regional resource officers to develop. Specific activities can emerge from projects and networks sharing common goals, including new sports clubs with opportunities for integrated activity and social and sports clubs where the emphasis is not purely on sport.

Longer term prospects for sport and recreation for people with a disability will continue to depend on financial support from a variety of agencies. The work of the Foundation for Sport and the Arts has confirmed that grant aid associated with opportunities for promoting and developing sport do lead to some exciting outcomes. The ten promotional videos on sport for people with disability from the Ideas Factory being one example. The establishment of a National Lottery, and further opportunities for significant grant aid, underlines a major need for all sports organisations to be well organised and prepared.

Perhaps it also confirms the necessity for a coordinated approach to satisfying need in sport and that the preparation of coherent strategies for sport based on collaboration between agencies is the best way forward. The prospect of one organisation representing diverse needs also has merit, particularly in times of economic constraints and competitive bids for grant aid.

Summary of key points

Six organisations involved with sport, have been selected from many others to provide a useful insight into selected aspects of management and development which affect or contribute towards a particular sport or recreation group.

1 The CCPR represents governing bodies in particular, and has established a focus on leadership.
2 The NCF seeks to service the needs of coaches, and governing bodies.
3 The ILAM is a professional institute representing those in leisure management. It has an important education and training and development function amongst many services to members.
4 Although the NPFA is essentially a resource oriented organisation, its objects are appreciated by managers and sports people everywhere. There is a clear difference between the five organisations and the NPFA but this should not conceal the fact that the NPFA does make a significant contribution in any debate on issues affecting outdoor facilities for British sport and recreation. This influence on policy makers, particularly in central and local government, is valued.
5 The SAF and the BSAD seek to assist the needs of two groups of sportsmen and women; the elite and those with a disability.
6 The CCPR, ILAM, NCF, NPFA, BSAD, SAF and the NPFA are all independent of the Sports Council and of government. Their ability to consider longer term plans must therefore be determined by the availability of sufficient resources. Finances are earned through services to members, contractual agreements with other organisations, grants and fund raising activities.
7 Resource generation, managing by objectives and satisfying the needs of particular groups or individuals are common priorities. The essential feature of the five organisations, as with the Sports Council, is that they have specific services to offer British sport. It is for managers to appreciate the contribution that independent organisations can make.
8 There is a rich assortment of non-governmental organisations that cannot be defined as governing bodies of sport but they make a significant contribution to the quality of British sport and recreation. The six organisations discussed in this chapter are each important but they are intended to serve as examples rather than to suggest a total picture.

References

1 The CCPR Annual Reports.
2 The Sports Council 1988 *Sport in the Community, Into the 90s*. P.75.
3 National Coaching Foundation 1992 *Annual Report 1992*.
4 The Sports Council 1990 *Coaching Matters*.
5 Institute of Leisure and Amenity Management 1992 *Annual Report 1991*. ILAM.
6 ILAM 1989 *Five Year Development Plan*.

7 *Sports Aid Foundation 1992 Sports Aid Foundation Annual Report 1991-92.* Sports Aid Foundation/Sports Aid Trust.
8 The National Playing Fields Association 1986 *Outdoor Playing Space Requirements, 6 Acre Target.*
9 The Sports Council 1982 *Sports Centres for Disabled People.*
10 BASD 1987 *BASD: A Five Year Plan.*
11 Greater London Association for the Disabled 1987 *Sport For All? A Report on Sports Opportunities for Disabled People in Greater London.*
12 Ian Elvin 1992 *Every Body Active, Coaching Scheme.* Research paper forthcoming.
13 Ian Elvin 1988 *Coaching and the Disabled, Every Body Active Working Paper.* Sunderland Polytechnic.
14 Yorkshire and Humberside RCSR, 1991 *Sport for People with Disabilities.* RCSR, Leeds.

Further reading

Evans, H. J. 1974 *Service to Sport, The Story of the CCPR 1935-1972.* The Sports Council, London.
NPFA 1991, *Annual Report and Accounts.*
School Sport Forum 1988 *Sport and Young People: Partnership and Action.* The Sports Council, London.
Simpson, S. 1989 *Sports Centres for Disabled People.* RADAR.
George Torkildsen 1992 *Leisure and Recreation Management.* Third Edition, Spon/E & F N Spon.

6 Governing bodies of sport

Introduction

With over 150,000 sports clubs in the UK, and 6.5 million members, the voluntary sector clearly plays a major part in the delivery of sporting opportunities.

Governing bodies of sport were, however, established to determine rules, organise and regulate competitions and to oversee national and international events.

Each sport has a unique profile of both historical origins and subsequent development. In the 1990s National Governing Bodies (NGBs) will be faced with a number of challenges, particularly related to resourcing. As organisations and agencies are placed under increasing financial pressure, sport will need to adapt. Whilst it is true that few sports are the same today as they were 20 years ago, the process of change is likely to accelerate. The need for improved management skills both at national and regional level will be necessary if specific objectives are to be realised. Cooperation between governing bodies and local authorities will need to be strengthened, particularly if the development of participation is a priority.

Relationships with other organisations are also likely to develop, expressly where there is mutual benefit in a relationship. Governing bodies of sport have a primary commitment to the development of performance and excellence. The technical know-how must also come from within the sports even if other forms of support or assistance come from willing partners.

One important responsibility that all NGBs have to their members is to be effective pressure groups when the need arises. Although the reasons for discontent may vary between sports the duty is delegated from clubs and individuals across the country. Small organisations cannot expect to influence the government or its agencies, but the executive officers have that task. It may be effected directly or through the CCPR.

The voluntary sector clubs may provide the backbone of British sport but we must also recognise the significance of professional sport. Although most participant sports remain largely amateur, it is certainly likely that professionalism, or the contribution of professional sports men and women, will help shape the character and the prospects of a sport. Over recent years, dramatic changes have taken place in certain sports largely due to the involvement of the media and the growth of sponsorship. Our major national sports have tried to develop a more market oriented approach, designed to maximise impact and income. Professional football, despite problems off the field, is attracting sponsors and continues to appeal to the television companies. Snooker, darts, boxing, squash, ice hockey and basketball each provide examples of indoor sports which illustrate a professional approach. The increase in popularity of snooker has owed much to the extent of television coverage and the emergence of a performing elite.

The influence of television, the media generally, and all the fame and wealth that it can bring to sports people also carries the possibility of corrupting the sport or the individuals who compete. Drugs, professionalism, codes of conduct, and event mismanagement are each matters of importance in modern sport. It may seem unfortunate that areas of difficulty can exist; however the governing body has a responsibility to all who participate, compete at a high level, or just spectate. Sports managers at local and regional level should seek and expect good and responsive communications with NGB executives. Governing bodies should be expected to manage their sports according to the requirements of their membership.

It is the outdoor sports, however, which enjoy so much popular support. Indeed, a number of these sports were first played in Britain to be taken around the world. As a nation we still expect to compete at the highest level in football, golf, athletics, cricket, rugby union, rugby league, sailing, rowing, bowls, hockey, motor racing and various equestrian sports. One has only to consider the hurt to our national pride that we cannot compete to the highest level in tennis, even though we organise one of the world's finest tennis tournaments, to understand the importance of sporting success.

Since a number of NGBs rely on major tournaments for the majority of financial input it is important to be successful. The international athletes, rugby players, cricketers and tennis players can rightly take some credit for the strength of their governing bodies. However there is also the problem that in order to establish a national elite NGBs need strategies, coaching schemes, and a support system for top sportsmen and sportswomen. They should also aim to be self-reliant for money. Grant aid is an attractive carrot but it can lead to specified constraints on behaviour. Sports Council grant can be tied to the implementation of a strategic plan for a governing body. If it is a critical source of grant, perhaps, necessary to survive in current form, NGBs would be advised to reflect on Sports Council and government policies.

Undoubtedly Britain can call on an increasing number of professional people who are salaried to a governing body. Responsibilities to NGBs include: coaching, development, administration, marketing and financial management. Of course there are salaried officers of NGBs who are not trained for the positions they now hold. There have been times when jobs were perhaps given to people only because of their previous international prowess. In the 1990s trained experienced professionals, who understand the needs of sport, will be more likely to assume positions of authority.

Table 6.1   The ten most popular sports in Great Britain, 1987, 1990

Persons aged 16 or over

Sport	1987 Millions	%	1990 Millions	%
	Adults participating in the 4 weeks before interview in the most popular quarter (MPQ).			
Walking	19.4	44	20.1	45
Swimming	8.5	19	9.8	22
Snooker/billiards/pool	6.9	16	6.2	14
KeepFit/yoga/aerobics	4.1	9	5.8	13
Cycling	4.5	10	4.9	11
Darts	4.8	11	3.6	8
Golf	2.7	6	3.1	7
Running (Jogging, X/C, road)	2.4	5	2.2	5
Weight training/lifting	2.2	5	2.1	5
Soccer	2.3	5	2.1	5
Base = 100%	19529		17574	

Sources: Matheson J 1991
Participation in Sport. Series GHS no 17.
OPCS 1992.

Governing bodies of sport will need to respond to growing pressures from central and local government, the Sports Council, grant aiding organisations, the media and commercial sponsors. Each sport will continue to illustrate a distinct profile even though mutual support should occasionally prove gainful. In order to consider further insight into specific issues you may wish to refer to sections in this text on the Sports Council, the CCPR, and the National Coaching Foundation.

The introduction of the National Non Domestic Rate in 1990 placed sports clubs in the voluntary sector on a business rate. Although offered a measure of protection over an interim period, sports organisations may, in the longer term, be required to pay an increased rate. Although local authorities can offer discretionary rate relief and make a substantial claim against central government resources (to the extent of 75 per cent of relief awarded) some local authorities are maintaining their 'no relief' policies. This will ultimately have an impact on the ability of sports clubs to offer an effective service to their local community. The CCPR continues to provide encouragement to sports clubs to request rate relief; however one of the difficulties faced in the early 1990s is that local authorities, faced with mounting constraints on their budgets, may find contributing even 25 per cent of the relief rather difficult. In order that voluntary sports clubs can receive necessary financial support a commitment must be made by government, both nationally and locally. Compulsory competitive tendering puts the availability of facilities at risk. The financial viability of some amateur sports organisations is under threat. Sports managers at local and regional level should recognise the problems and work with the governing bodies accordingly.

With falling numbers of young adults in prospect through the early 1990s NGBs must turn their attention towards:

1 Preparing, delivering and monitoring a corporate strategy which includes meaningful objectives.
2 Attracting more people (of various backgrounds) into sport. These should include administrators and players.
3 Developing partnerships with other organisations based on mutual needs and benefits.
4 Offering the media, and television in particular, a well formed product. The image of a sport in the eyes of the consumer will be pre-eminent. Even though the sport might be for the players, it has been established that some changes may have to occur to satisfy the media.
5 Encouraging sponsorship and the benefits to sponsors will become increasingly important. Sport cannot take the money and run. Proper business relationships will need to be based on a clear understanding of roles and responsibilities.
6 Enhancing self reliance based on a portfolio of skills and commitments. Training administrators, developing partnerships, attracting media and sponsors will only offer part of an answer. NGBs will be required to operate effectively and efficiently before they can attract the necessary resources.
7 Through organisations like the CCPR the NGBs must apply pressure on the policy makers. Without continual pressure NGBs may:
   - enjoy fewer outdoor playing facilities
   - need to pay a 'commercial rate' for facilities used
   - pay higher levels of National Non Domestic Rate
   - continue to account to central government regarding current levels of Corporation Tax, PAYE, trust funds, professional sportsmen and women and Value Added Tax (VAT)

Although sports clubs and governing bodies rely on enormous amounts of goodwill and unpaid labour, prospects for the 1990s seem to suggest that a system of stronger, fitter and more objective organisations will be necessary.

National and regional governing bodies are increasingly likely to find that the management of their sport becomes more complicated, imposes greater demands on their time and is more resource oriented. Whilst training schemes and education programmes are available for managers in other sectors it seems likely that NGBs will have to develop appropriate training schemes for senior staff, or recruit professional managers in preference to retired performers who lack the management skills. Where expertise does not exist, or where there is merit in working with other agencies, like the NCF, a responsive style of management is required.

Issues affecting selected outdoor sports

Whereas ownership of outdoor sports facilities falls within both the public and private sectors, it is the National Governing Bodies who have contributed so much to the quantity and quality of our sporting traditions. Operationally they contribute at a different level to local clubs focusing primarily on competitions, events and the development of excellence. Voluntary organisations are significant providers of facilities in certain sports, especially golf and cricket. Local authorities may own and supply facilities for sports such as tennis, football and athletics but it is the local clubs and members who actually service the needs of members, participate in the competitions, deliver the coaching and provide the required social environment.

The basis upon which much of British sport is organised comes from voluntary unpaid labour. This applies to governing bodies and local clubs. Trends in sports participation and pressures of work have, however, resulted in an increasing number of full-time paid administrators. Financial considerations determine the viability of such positions; indeed not all sports have been fortunate enough to create the necessary posts.

Table 6.2 Ten largest Governing Bodies of Sport in 1989

	Members 000s
English Golf Union	501
National Federation of Anglers	285
Scottish Golf Union	149
English Bowling Association	132
British Crown Green Bowling Association	128
English Karate	110
English Ladies' Golf Association	107
British Association for Shooting and Conservation	105
Scottish Bowling Association	92
Badminton Association of England	90

Source: National Governing Bodies, 1989.

Sports governing bodies cater for those who are individual members or affiliated through clubs. Sportsmen and women on the other hand need not be members of a club, although in certain sports it is difficult not to be. To play golf on one of the privately owned courses one has to join a club or, alternatively, be a member of another club and pay a green fee for temporary membership. Casual play in golf is otherwise largely restricted to pay as you play courses and local authority facilities. In Scotland, recognised for good provision, only 15 per cent of courses are managed by local authorities. Only club members can be awarded a handicap and only those with a handicap can play in a competition. Golf is not typical of all sports or activities. It is possible to participate in a number of outdoor activities without being a club member including:

Club membership *not* essential (outdoor sports)

Walking, including rambling	Horse riding
Swimming	Sailing
Fishing	Canoeing
Cycling	Surfing
Tennis	Skiing
Bowls	Climbing/potholing

Each of these sports is represented by a National Governing Body, regional associations and clubs. Indeed some activities have more than one governing body.

The list seeks only to represent some of the more popular sports. Other sports activity can only take place on an informal, recreational basis unless an individual, or a group of individuals, are club members. Participation in any kind of organised competition or event is normally the bench mark for needing to become a club member.

Club membership *essential* (outdoor sports)

Football	Golf
Athletics	Hockey
Cricket	Rugby

Without belonging to a formal organisation it is difficult to play in a recognised game or enter a bona fide event.

Six sports have been selected to provide a little insight into the diversity and complexity of the organisations and issues involved in outdoor sports. The well established sports of cycling, angling, orienteering, mountaineering, caving and rambling also offer very different challenges and opportunities to the participant.

Cycling

Governing bodies, regional bodies and clubs exert influence or control over much of their sport but their authority is not total. Many people participate in a recreational activity without seeking governing body membership. For instance cycling involves the British Cycling Federation (BCF) as the governing body for sport; the Road Time Trials Council (RTTC) looks after cycle time trialing; the British Cyclo Cross Association (BCA), the Cyclists Touring Club (CTC), the representative Cycling Council of Britain (dealing with common issues), the Cycle Speedway Council (CSC), the UK BMX Association, the Scottish Cyclists Union (SCU) and the Northern Ireland Cycling Federation (NICF). Add to this impressive list one organisation representing the manufacturers and one representing retailers and the list is nearly complete.

Over one million people cycle, yet the NGBs actually represent only those in membership. The BCF has some 860 affiliated clubs and 15,000 members, while the CTC has over 38,000 members and is Britain's largest national cycling organisation.

Each of the cycling governing bodies exists to carry out a role and exercise certain duties. They are not necessarily in conflict with each other or with cyclists who are not in membership.[1]

Angling

Angling, in one form or another, comes under the influence of a number of governing bodies. It is the National Angler's Council (NAC) who is responsible for the sport in England and Wales. The four foundation members of the NAC include: The Fishmonger's Company, The National Federation of Anglers, The National Federation of Sea Anglers and The Salmon and Trout Association. Scotland has no overall governing body while Wales has some autonomy from the NAC. The NAC is responsible for coaching but there is no schools' organisation.[3]

After walking and swimming, angling is one of the most popular sports. Over three million anglers, including one million who fish once per month, enjoy a variety of sporting applications including: bait fishing, fly fishing, spinning, coarse, sea or game fishing. Not all anglers are in club membership which makes accurate prediction of future trends difficult.

A sport that is dominated by men from diverse professional and trade positions also has regional variances or preferences. It experiences pressures on finite resources, potential conflict with other recreational pursuits, pollution and access. Major issues identified by the NAC include canoes, access, bait digging problems in sea angling and grant aid

Table 6.3 Trends in club membership-angling

	1965	1970	1975	1980	1981	1982	1983	1984	1985
National Federation of Anglers									
Number of affiliated associations	113	152	265	374	392	404	417	423	431
Number of members of associations	439500	403000	451000	478000	452981	407773	392134	356234	332934
National Federation of Sea Anglers									
Number of affiliated clubs	185	607	504	773	–	–	–	–	–
Number of personal members	250	590	850	1200	–	–	–	–	–
The Salmon and Trout Association									
Number of affiliated clubs									120
Number of members of clubs									10000
Scottish Federation of Anglers									
Number of affiliated clubs								130	120
Number of individual members								300	350
Scottish Anglers National Association									
Number of affiliated clubs and associations									380
Number of individual members									100
Welsh Federation of Sea Anglers									
Number of affiliated clubs			773	753	787	727	647	–	–
Number of individual members				1200	1160	983	879	846	–
Ulster Angling Federation									
Number of affiliated clubs					27	28	–	30	32
Number of individual members					2846	3250	–	4240	5224
Ulster Coarse Fishing Federation									
Number of affiliated clubs					15	15	12	12	11
Number of individual members					900	1000	850	1000	1030
Ulster Council of the Irish Federation of Anglers									
Number of affiliated clubs					76	86	82	67	68
Number of individual members					1520	–	1640	1245	1315

difficulties. The most serious matter facing anglers follows the privatisation of the water industry and the establishment of a National River Authority. The NRA, in assuming responsibility for regulatory and river basin functions, becomes accountable for river management functions of flood defence, drainage, fisheries, recreation and water quality. The utility functions of the water industry become the responsibility of ten public companies. The NRA will have a significant role although it can call on the support of the Regional Fisheries Advisory Committees (RFACs).

NRAs must have regard to the conservation of the environment and promote access for recreation wherever possible. Issues that also effect the sport of angling include the cost of illegal poaching and who should pay for law enforcement. There is a strong argument that this responsibility should not fall on the law-abiding angler. The ability or the willingness of local authorities to award discretionary rate reductions to help angling and other sporting clubs is a topic of wide interest. The NAC, however, openly declares its support for the NRA and its objectives, although certain reservations exist.

More specific and localised problems, such as the discharge of untreated sewage and the effect of drift netting, are pursued by The Salmon and Trout Association. Seen by some to be an elitist group, the Association provides one example of an organisation's involvement in the management of affairs affecting their sport. Encouraging farmers, land owners, the companies managing our water supply and the government to consider the effects of industry on the environment is one ongoing matter, as is the need for a dialogue between different governing bodies all competing for the same space. There are some influential members amongst the Association's 150 clubs and 100,000 anglers which makes the promotion of meaningful dialogue a little easier to cultivate.

Caving

So many sports in Britain today are anxious to promote participation and development, but there are genuine difficulties when participation is not dependent on being a member of a club, or affiliated to a national governing body. Not only are illegal poaching and conflict between sports using the same environment constant problems, there is also the health and safety risk by non-registered sports people. The National Caving Association (NCA) seeks development through recognised clubs so that conservation of caves, proper training and the development of appropriate equipment can become priorities. Access, closely related to conservation, is the greatest concern of the NCA, although concern exists regarding the possible loss of facilities through either quarrying or the dumping of waste materials.[4]

The NCA is a federation of existing regional Councils of Caving Clubs plus the five established organisations responsible for one aspect of caving. These are the British Association of Caving Instructors, the British Cave

Rescue Council, the British Cave Research Association, The William Pengedy Cave Studies Trust Ltd and the Cave Diving Group.

One example of regional Councils comes from the Council of Northern Caving Clubs which has certain anxieties. The last 30 years have witnessed a change in attitudes by farmers towards cavers and caving. Although farmers may have understandable reservations over the numbers of people accessing their land and any inherent risk to the environment, particularly by less qualified or non-affiliated sports people, a solution has yet to be found. With legal uncertainty concerning access to the countryside and landowner's liability, negotiating permitted access has been difficult. The Council of Northern Caving Clubs recognises that this has resulted in clandestine visits to caves which, in most cases, have been known to the farmer although it is believed that a request for permission however would be denied. It was this access difficulty in fact which lead to the Council of Northern Caving Clubs being established in 1963. The NCA has taken the difficulties recognised at a regional level and some progress, through legislation, looks likely.

Orienteering

Orienteering increasingly faces land access problems, just as the effects of orienteering on the environment have come under scrutiny. Not only are new restrictions and conditions being imposed, but more landlords are actually making a financial charge in return for access permission. The British Orienteering Federation (BOF) is opposing an access charge and, with concern for the environment, is carrying out its own study. However, with membership increasing and club activity growing, the BOF should be confident of the future. Clearly access difficulties require the Governing Body's close attention, as does the ability to raise sponsorship, generate publicity (common difficulties) and persuade the Sports Council of the worthiness of the sport's development plan. So much has happened since 1965 when the English Orienteering Association was formed, with Chris Basher as Chairman.

The BOF followed two years later with the World Championships coming to Scotland in 1976. By 1987 the sport had grown to 150 clubs, 6,500 members and 1300 events.[5] Orienteering in Britain is now well organised and well established. As growth presumably continues, the BOF will continue to play an important role. Not only will the 'Forward Plan' demand a significant commitment, focusing on participation, coaching, competitions, mapping, excellence and international affairs, but the previously discussed matter of access arrangements is likely to grow in importance. As with a number of other sports the future development of orienteering, along with Sports Council grant aid, has become a vital factor. Sponsorship, so important to the major sports, is also a necessary feature of BOF activity, particularly in organising major events. The problem will be, however, to attract sufficient sponsorship into a sport that has as yet to attract major media interest.

Mountaineering

The British Mountaineering Council (BMC) also concedes that the Sports Council grant, linked to the BMC three year development plan, has had a real impact.[6] Similar BMC issues arise to those of the BOF and NCA, namely threats to the environment and access difficulties. Another common problem comes from so many climbers not belonging to a recognised club. Compulsory competitive tendering (CCT) may, according to the BMC, affect the provision and use of climbing walls in that they involve considerable investment for a minimal return. With increasing membership and full member clubs containing approximately 30,000 members, prospects look healthy. Encouragement by the CCPR for outdoor pursuits and adventure activity is starting to bring benefits. Membership on National Park Committees is a real encouragement as is the CCPR inspired Community Sport Leaders Expedition Award. The BMC, in representing all who take part in mountaineering activity, will continue to have an important role in training, technical evaluation, access agreements, artificial climbing walls, and international affairs.

Rambling

The Ramblers Association, in common with so many governing bodies involved in outdoor activities, expresses its greatest concerns as access, and opportunity for recreation.[7] Not only can rambling boast three times as many participants as the next most popular outdoor activity, swimming, but many of those involved take part on a regular basis. However in its paper, *Make for the Hills*, the argument is firmly made that:

> government officials, local authorities and public bodies show a distinct lack of interest in securing adequate access to open country and improving recreation opportunities, even though access can often be provided at relatively low cost.[8]

Pressures on land use come not only from recreationists. Agriculture continues to exert considerable political and economic influence. The conversion of Moorland to enclose agricultural land, the afforestation of our uplands, and the loss of semi-natural deciduous woodlands have resulted in a significant change to our countryside. The military make extensive use of some of our wilderness areas, including Dartmoor and the Northumberland National Park. Not only does the RA believe that recreation and other land use in the uplands are not in serious conflict, there are also proposals to ensure a continuing respect for these areas. A strategy for quiet recreation in upland areas includes encouraging access, the promotion of management agreements, a greater financial input from government, better public transport, more inexpensive accommodation and proper representation on all public bodies involved in the uplands. The Ramblers Association Annual Report of 1991 acknowledges the Rights of Way Act 1990, but deplores the failure of local councils to enforce the Act.[9] The RA continues to press for legislation concerning common land. Rights of way in England and Wales can still be difficult to walk as a result of ploughing or other forms of cultivation, the disappearance of 4000 miles of hedgerow every year and the extensive use of pesticides and the problem is clear to see. Our countryside is a heritage worthy of greater planning control. With the privatisation of water, concern can only grow for the retention of rights of public access to the countryside.

The efforts of the RA can only have a limited effect given the strength of the farming lobby and the prevailing political emphasis in favour of economic land use. Indeed the political influence of groups with an environmental role is in part determined by their own ability to employ sufficient resources.

Summary of key points

1 Outdoor sports make considerable demands on finite resources. Conflicting pressures on land use certainly create problems for central and local government and voluntary organisations.

2 The UK enjoys a rich assortment of outdoor sports, a number of which are seen as major participant activities. The preceding examples of walking (rambling), angling and cycling are known as important in a British cultural context. Caving, canoeing, orienteering and mountaineering are also important in their own right and they keenly demonstrate the importance of good access arrangements. Conflict between vested interests in sport, or anywhere else for that matter, remains inevitable.

3 Cooperation, coordination and an element of compromise are always likely to have a productive outcome for those organisations and managers who are willing to both talk and listen. Promoting sport does not require the surrendering of values. Conservation of natural resources, for example, is an issue which continues to affect sports men and women. For many sports participants, conservation is a major factor which they will defend. This is especially true in the more remote areas of our countryside.

4 Governing bodies serve an important function as pressure groups and as agents of development. They act as a barrier to misplaced proposals for land development and they stimulate growth in participation.

Issues affecting selected indoor sports

An appreciation of some organisational opportunities and constraints relating to badminton, table tennis and lawn tennis provides a contrasting perspective to those sports which rely less on built facilities. Each activity presents issues that seek to confirm the tremendously varied nature of sport in the UK. In order to effect reasonable comparison, the following case studies adopt a similar style of presentation.

The selected sports of badminton and table tennis will each illustrate a profile which introduces the organisation, facility provision, resource management including sponsorship, coach and player development and an appraisal of current management issues.

Lawn tennis has been chosen as a sport seeking actively to encourage facility development. An outline feasibility study of an Indoor Tennis Initiative scheme will challenge the manager to consider a thorough approach to sports provision.

There is a danger in writing about one sport in which you are not involved. The selection of all case study material therefore is used for illustrative purposes. It is the broad functions, the relationships and the developments for the future that are of interest to a wider audience and it is to those issues that the contents of this text are addressed.

Case study: Badminton Association of England (BAE)

Introduction
1993 is the centenary year for the Badminton Association of England. Interestingly the BAE itself was formed in 1934 out of the Badminton Association formed in 1893. The English Schools Badminton Association was established in 1965 and is affiliated to the BAE. There are separate governing bodies in Scotland and Wales. Ulster is a part of the Badminton Union of Ireland.

Badminton is the sixth most popular indoor sport with slightly fewer numbers than squash. Estimates from the BAE suggest one million regular players although it is likely that there may well be another 1.5 million occasional players.

Facilities
The growth of indoor leisure centres in the 1970s and 1980s has enabled much more casual (recreational) badminton to take place. Individuals do not have to affiliate or join a club in order to play the game. The effect of this would appear to be more people playing badminton but a reduced number affiliating to the governing body. Governing bodies exist for the benefit of the game and its members. Although the development of local authority facilities has encouraged people to play badminton the BAE has failed to attract them into membership.

School halls and dual use provision continue to provide an important contribution to the playing of badminton. When examining the use made of indoor sports halls, participation in badminton competes for space against alternative sports provision. A hall might equally service the needs of volleyball, tennis, five-a-side football or basketball. As compulsory competitive tendering and a more cost effective approach to management becomes increasingly important, decisions will be made by facility owners regarding the most 'profitable' use of space. It is not simply a question of how many people can be accommodated in a hall, but how much can they pay. Currently badminton is a fairly low cost activity but it can and does generate more income per court hour than some sports.

Although the sport has potential and attracts reasonable income, compulsory competitive tendering poses some doubts as to future pricing policies in local authority centres. This, along with a lack of available community-based courts and a declining membership, presents a dilemma for those who support badminton. The governing body and local authority officers, as with other activities, needed to build in provision for the game in tender specifications. Pressure will need to be applied in order that the game maintains current court space and time. Club membership and affiliation are a more complex matter but one would expect membership of any organisation to offer benefits. School-based facilities provide an important opportunity to play the game, but it is also necessary to provide the coaching and competitive experience if youngsters are to remain interested. In recent years a pattern is emerging, governing body coaches are going into schools to assist with sports development.

Resource Management

Since the development of an elite also requires a broad base of participation the BAE is taking a positive stance to the future.

The annual reports continue to confirm the importance of two major items of income. Sponsorship of the All England Championship was essential as was the significant grant aid from the Sports Council. As with so many governing bodies, the generation of sponsorship money is vital. Promoting a national or international championship is not enough to attract large sponsorship. It is becoming more and more necessary to attract media attention, particularly television.

As with many sports or recreation organisations the ability to attract sufficient income is tremendously important. The image a game has can come from participation in school, the appeal of the game in a local sports centre, impressions from television coverage or from the personalities involved. A sustained effort to develop participation and remain solvent must be based on cost effective programmes. To this end governing bodies must think and act aggressively. Partnerships with other organisations will be necessary, particularly if resources cannot sustain a large staff infrastructure: the development of local clubs and schools, district recreation departments and local education authorities, and regional or national companies with sponsorship potential.

Coach and player development

In order to sustain impetus there must be a structure which supports increased participation. Badminton has adopted a decentralised coaching structure which is allied to player development and operates at two levels. Developments in performance must occur within a well organised and clearly defined structure. One partnership established between the BAE and the NCF will offer education support for coach development. Coaches are required to attend NCF courses at regional centres based on a selection prescribed by the governing body. With badminton now an Olympic sport the future looks exciting providing the strategy for development succeeds.

Current management issues

Some of the regional and national priorities have been identified albeit at a policy level. Underpining the BAE's approach to the future is a plan to expand in four major areas:

1   Increase in mass participation by greater involvement with primary schools. The BAE will not be alone in reaching out for young people. Although the primary schools may welcome support the issue of coaches working with youngsters should involve LEA advisors, headteachers and parents. Coaches may need a training programme which identifies and tackles the different working relationships to those normally employed in a badminton club.
2   Increase opportunities for coaching especially in the performance category. In forming a link with the NCF the BAE has already adopted a shared approach to what could be a major exercise. Local authorities are major providers of facilities for badminton. The casual player who uses these centres might appreciate some coaching or the opportunity to coach. A shared approach aimed at developing performance and coaching could satisfy the centre managers and the governing body. Contract management, in a post CCT environment, should require educational and coaching programmes if the quality, and perhaps quantity, of sports participation is not going to suffer.
3   Increase in involvement with technical/coach events in Europe to help to

improve already identified excellence at age group level. It is probably at the level of the elite performer that governing bodies will need to search hardest for financial support and for partners who can assist. Potential sponsors must see the benefits of a package. There may be a European initiative suitable for actually developing this dimension which, for example, neighbouring governing bodies and European companies might wish to be associated with.

4 Increase, by at least four, the number of Teacher Award Courses. Any attempt to reach into schools is much more likely to succeed if the teachers themselves are supportive and can assist. As with so many sports award courses and qualifications, providing a follow up service might ensure that those with qualifications can and actually do promote the game. Potential for this award should be pursued in schools, colleges and institutions of higher education, sports centre staff and those with approved experience.

Conclusion

A number of issues have been identified which are highly significant for managers and which go far wider than the governing body itself. Although the value of working with others has been identified it should be recognised that the main objective is the satisfaction of governing body goals which are themselves an integral part of their strategy. In this regard the BAE is little different from other agencies covered in this text. The biggest exercise might be to share the discussion on strategic development with local authorities (education and recreation), and organisations like the NCF.

Case study: English Table Tennis Association (ETTA)

In addition to the ETTA there is an English Schools Table Tennis Association, the Scottish Table Tennis Association (STTA), the Table Tennis Association of Wales (TTAW) and the Ulster branch of the Irish Table Tennis Association (UBITTA). The ETTA established in 1921, is the governing body for men and women in England.

The objectives of the ETTA essentially cover the laws of the game, the legislative authority, the responsibility for promotion and development of table tennis in England, and a supporting role to the International Table Tennis Federation.[11]

Table tennis became an Olympic sport in 1988 and at the same time enjoyed greater coverage from British television.

One of the problems all NGBs must face, including table tennis, is how to determine success. Even with a well documented development plan, various criteria can emerge as critical in assessing performance namely:

1 Achievements in national and international competitions.
2 Developments in domestic competitions, including greater participation.
3 Increased television and media coverage for the sport.
4 More sponsorship money coming into the sport.
5 Improved financial performance over a given period.
6 Successful grass roots coaching development schemes.
7 Combination of 1-6 according to a well constructed development plan.

These seven points illustrate issues that face many managers. Managing by objectives stresses the need for quantifiable targets. Levels of excellence in competitions can be measured by the number of trophies that are won. Participation targets can be assessed by the number of people taking part. This could apply equally to coaching. Financial measures of performance are essentially quantitative but more objective data can be used to complement traditional methods. Ratio analysis uses simple techniques to relate expenditure against performance targets. Although the ratios must be used advisedly they are a useful tool for managers.

Difficulties emerge when factors change which are outside the managers' control. A sponsor withdraws, a competition is put at risk, the television company pulls out, and the revenue for a coaching scheme disappears. The world of sport management is rapidly facing up to increased pressures and the importance of satisfying objectives.

Facilities

Table tennis enjoys one clear advantage over many traditional sports. The game does not require expensive facilities or equipment. Local halls can function as well as a large sports complex for a game that attracts approximately 700,000 adults plus a significant number of children.

The ETTA introduced a scheme, Bounce into Action, in an attempt to attract leisure centre users into club membership. A similar ambition has previously been discussed in relation to badminton.

Demands on time and space need not be great. Centre managers should find the programming of table tennis relatively straight forward.

Local authorities as providers and enablers, local clubs and the regional or national associations in sharing similar goals should forge even better partnerships if continued progress is to be maintained. The 'abolition funds' made available in the Metropolitan County Councils provided an illustration of this. A project based in Tyne and Wear, which focused on a wide table tennis programme of activity, worked with Newcastle, Gateshead, Sunderland, North Tyneside and South Tyneside – all participating with both financial and resource support. The Sports Council-based funding has above all else demonstrated the value of working together. Partnerships and sharing schemes should be considered across local authority boundaries.

Table tennis, however, has lost a significant number of its membership in recent years. Although the decline has been reduced to something under five per cent, it is a worrying factor. On the one hand recreational activity seems to be fairly significant but clubs do not seem to enjoy the benefits. This factor can also be identified in badminton, squash and tennis. Table tennis has increased membership in a number of leagues to offset some of the anxiety but reports suggest that television exposure and national publicity is what is really needed to improve matters radically. Table tennis clubs would need to determine sustainable levels of membership. Since the game is easily incorporated into a wide range of facilities, it requires a very broad based approach at regional and district level if participation levels and club developments are to be successful. Once again we arrive at the chicken and egg situation. More money is required to develop the game but until the resources are available it is difficult to make progress.

Resource management

Governing bodies are in the main achieving financial viability with small balances going into reserve accounts. Table tennis is no exception and the sport requires a well constructed management plan. Since 1987, accounts have been computerised with a regular supply of data including an analysis of performance against heads of spending. Control, however, is only one dimension. Money has to be earned in order that it can be spent.

Sponsorship has provided the ETTA with an excellent opportunity to promote the game. When two tournaments cost 100,000 to put on, the value of a sponsorship deal is immense. In 1987 the Leeds Permanent Building Society took over the sponsorship of the majority of the Association's tournament activities for three years. The 500,000 sponsorship package was linked to Alan Pascoe Associates Limited, which had previously worked with the ETTA as consultants. The Leeds has also funded two regionally based projects and Eagle Star has produced two coaching video tapes. Sponsorship became tremendously important to many governing bodies in the late 1980s, and it is anticipated that there is much more to come. In the interests of table tennis it is hoped that they are successful in attracting sponsors and television coverage.

The interesting question here is, to what extent should NGBs commit themselves to sponsorship deals? If the game does not generate sufficient resources sponsorship may be one answer, but it comes with a price. There is always the risk of major sponsors withdrawing from an event. With sponsorship commanding a high profile, as in table tennis, organisations are bound to consider whether or not they have the professional expertise to deliver what is necessary. Using recognised commercial organisations to attract sponsorship offers benefits but the NGB's ambition might be to bring the activity in house and employ their own sponsorship experts.

Sports managers who organise events, and attract sponsors, have often dealt with budgets which see all the sponsors' money spent on the event itself, including prizes, with no financial return to the organising body. In fact when this is set against the tremendous amount of work required, perhaps some of it on overtime payments there is a need for caution. The advice for governing bodies is the same for sports managers: be clear why you seek sponsorship and what your organisation wishes to get from it. A clearly defined item within the strategy document should make the position known.

The overall message from table tennis is similar to that from badminton. Firm and clear management principles need to guide the work of the governing bodies and sports managers elsewhere.

Coach and player development

Bounce into Action, club leagues, trials and cup competitions form the basis for local initiatives. Cuts in the coaching scheme were effected following an overspend in 1987. Following a reduction in professional staff, the emphasis was placed on involving volunteer coaches. The result was the appointment of 65 Regional Coaches. Development of table tennis will be through Regional Coaches, Centres of Excellence, Advanced Training Centres, League club and school coaching, Coaching awards, Junior development and skills awards.

Table tennis has become an Olympic sport, just like badminton. This may open up exciting new opportunities for media exposure and sponsorship. All sports however should recognise that long term developments are based on a plan which makes careful note of important elements, e.g. coaching, excellence, and grass roots participation, in other words a healthy infrastructure. One of the problems facing many sports clubs today is that they lack the personnel to perform those duties which are important for the future. The role of leaders, coaches and managers is accepted. An additional need seems to be for willing trained administrators, who may even be volunteers.

Table tennis is seeking to devolve responsibility to 65 regional coaches. With diminishing resources at a national level this decision might have been made for the ETTA by its own bank account. Time will tell if it was the correct solution. With a healthy regard for the future, a commitment should be made to a grass roots scheme and to the continued development of a training programme.

Current management issues

Table tennis, like badminton, wishes to attract new players, and their membership subscriptions. A similar situation exists for many facility managers who seek the right image for a game and view selective marketing as fundamental.

The ability to succeed in sport, and in managing a business, is based on recognising the strengths and weaknesses of the organisation and on making the most of the opportunities that the market offers.

The quality and depth of English table tennis is partly due to the governing bodies' coaching model. Regular monitoring of performance will assist in the evaluation of targets. If resources are needed to achieve meaningful targets do not be afraid to collaborate with like minded authorities and agencies.

Just as participation data assists the regular review process, a simple but fast system of financial control can also ensure up-to-date information for on the spot decisions.

Conclusion

In attempting to use specific sports to highlight advice to a wider audience it is inevitable that some items will be missed and others perhaps exaggerated. Table tennis in England does lend itself to one fairly wide ranging comment. When planning ahead, in any aspect of sport, consider what information will be required to judge performance. Whether the data is financial, or based on levels of participation, managers should determine the timing of this feedback and the possible options open to them.

Case study: Lawn Tennis Association (LTA)

Having provided two short case studies of specific National Governing Bodies, to illustrate some wide ranging management issues, this section will profile very different topics at a micro level. This study will feature the Lawn Tennis Association and its commitment to the development of indoor tennis. The character of the exercise also suggests that local authorities, local voluntary organisations and commercial companies will have an interest in future facility development.

To understand fully the relationship between the encouragement of tennis and the Indoor Tennis Initiative, a brief background to the growth of the game will be useful. The Lawn Tennis Association (LTA) is now over 100 years old, having been formed in 1888. Tennis is one of our most popular summer games, with participation reaching 1,250,000 adults and children. There are approximately 2,500 LTA affiliated clubs with 250,000 members.[13]

Two management issues arise here. With most facilities outdoors and only suited to playing in the summer months, participation is largely spasmodic. This does not encourage mass participation or the development of excellence. The development of more indoor facilities has therefore become an important priority for the LTA and local authorities.

The seasonality of tennis and the popular expectation of cheap sport means that clubs often do not generate enough subscription income per court. Facility development is often a financial impossibility for clubs.

Tennis courts in the public sector are an important asset but the economic difficulties of the last decade have seen many fall into disrepair. Poor surfaces produce poor sport. Neglected and vandalised courts have even become unusable. Managers must therefore decide if the game is to be encouraged and at what price. Is remedial work on tarmac surfaces sufficient or should we recognise the overriding inadequacies and develop indoor tennis? Here the problem seems to be that, although local authorities may own the courts, they do not have the financial resources to pay for new or refurbished facilities. To take the debate one stage further, even if money were available, who is going to be responsible for the management and operation of an indoor tennis centre? This could well be a further financial burden.

The LTA is a relatively strong governing body and with the benefits of over 11 million pa contribution from the All England Lawn Tennis Club Championships at Wimbledon it is in a position to make some investment in facility provision.

Lawn tennis became an Olympic sport in 1988, but if Britain continues to offer a poor level of facility we remain unlikely medal winners. The encouragement of participation also depends on the availability of a development plan. The LTA

Volkswagen rating scheme, increased sponsorship, the National League and signs of improvement in some of our elite players provides the basis for encouragement.

In order that the game might enjoy a prosperous future the LTA has prepared and published a Corporate Plan. One aspect of this plan is the encouragement of Indoor Tennis Initiative Centres. ITI involves cooperation, partnerships and a realistic attitude to the short- and medium-term future. Because it involves a variety of public and private sector agencies, the issues involved are of direct relevance to sport and recreation managers.

The next few pages will develop an outline of a feasibility study of an Indoor Tennis Initiative Centre in Newcastle Upon Tyne. Any large town can act as a substitute here since the arguments are based on sports, social and economic principles. A profile of how a manager might prepare and present an ITI proposal is also entirely relevant to a number of issues affecting the game of tennis and the management of sports in general.

Indoor tennis initiative

The city of Newcastle-Upon-Tyne aims to provide leisure facilities for all sections of the community and to maximise use of these facilities. The potential effect of rate capping which restricts expenditure, and the consequences of CCT place a firm constraining influence on local authority managers. Not only must they meet their social objectives, but they must also show that schemes involving the development of sport are financially viable.

The Lawn Tennis Association launched the ITI as its response to a clearly identified problem. Indoor centres needed to offer tennis on a pay-as-you-play basis, linked to community programmes, and operating over a full calendar year. The LTA further proposed that the development of facilities should be on local authority owned land. A long lease would be sufficient.

The local authority would develop a community scheme with LTA support. Grant aid of 33 per cent for facility development could be complemented by a 50 per cent grant towards the cost of a Tennis Development Officer for three years. LTA support would further extend to professional and technical advice, national advertising and promotional support and an activities manual.

A feasibility study is necessary if managers are to feel at all confident about the decision making process. ITIs in St Albans, Warrington, Sunderland and Swansea are operational; others are being developed. Encouraging early successes in these schemes are worthy of close scrutiny by local authorities which declare an interest. The LTA will continue to develop its own professional expertise as new centres are opened.

An ITI in Newcastle-Upon-Tyne

However hard one examines schemes in other centres of population there must be a keen emphasis placed on the feasibility of a local proposal. In 1989 only three indoor centres existed in the North East of England. Apart from the ITI Centre in Sunderland there were private centres in Middlesbrough and at Teeside airport. These three centres are not readily accessible to people living on Tyneside. Teeside and Middlesbrough are each over 40 miles distant and the centre in Sunderland is about 15 miles from Newcastle-Upon-Tyne.

The LTA recommends a catchment area for indoor facilities of 20,000 people living within a 20 mile drive. With a population of about 250,000 in Newcastle and with the neighbouring populations of North Tyneside, South Tyneside and Gateshead there was real scope for developing the idea further.

There is just one indoor centre in Newcastle-Upon-Tyne at the Northumberland club, which is used exclusively by members and elite training squads.

Following the early consideration of facilities in competition, the required catchment area, and existing levels of local sports facility provision, it is important to develop a demand assessment. Work is therefore required to prepare a report which not only examines current levels of participation, at all ages, including education provision, but also seeks to determine levels of latent demand for tennis.

Researching such a proposal would also need a detailed investigation into location, development and financial viability. Some prestige schemes around the country have struggled. It is vital that ITI centres are located in the right place and that they are managed to realistic and viable usage levels.

Feasibility studies must be logical, methodical, sequential and sufficiently demanding that managers at local authority, governing body or even club level can feel confident about reaching a decision. That decision should relate to a clear view on whether or not a specific centre should proceed.

At an early stage in the feasibility process there should be a meeting between the LTA and the local authority. Further meetings should be held with the local tennis clubs. An ITI is very likely going to be of interest to them. It is conceivable that one club may even seek actively to support the development. A further partnership, between club, local authority and the LTA, is possible, providing the criteria and objectives for an ITI can be met. Figure 6.1 illustrates this.

Figure 6.1   Partnership between LAs and LTAs

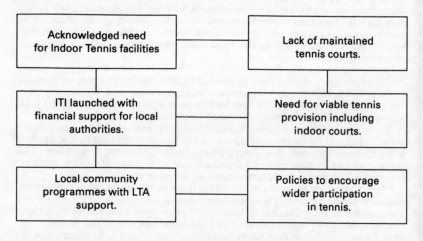

Already it can be seen that the prospect of facility development should involve managers and administrators from a number of organisations.

In pursuing the feasibility study, information is needed from a number of local sources including: locally elected councillors; Northumberland LTA; Newcastle-Upon-Tyne Local Education and Leisure Departments; local tennis clubs; Newcastle's tennis in the parks scheme; the local rates office; and the local authority planning officer. Each of these organisations and individuals will have a perception of need, priority and viability.

Selection of site
In any urban environment the possible areas for facility development are limited. The study needs to focus on an area of council-owned land that could be used for at least three indoor and three outdoor tennis courts, plus the necessary infrastructure of access, parking and services. Ideally, maps and ward profiles should be available to provide instant information.

The Castle Farm site, known as Paddy Freemans, in Newcastle-Upon-Tyne, was chosen for further investigation. A study of the location involved analysis of the catchment area including a neighbourhood survey, examination of location infrastructure and a survey of building options.

Following this investigation it was confirmed that Paddy Freemans would be a suitable site because:

1 It was land owned by the local authority.
2 The catchment area satisfied the LTAs needs.
3 Access to the area was easy from the city centre.
4 Public transport was regular and adjacent.
5 There was no local competition.
6 The site had full potential for development, including car parking.

Not only is it important for managers to appreciate the need for information it is also necessary to specify some qualitative data.

Assessing general demand can be achieved by a representative sample of the Newcastle population. Before spending a lot of time on this it is worth checking to see if related pieces of research have been carried out by other agencies, institutions or individuals. In fact locally-based research in Newcastle-Upon-Tyne confirmed a positive attitude towards tennis and higher than anticipated levels of participation during the summer months on outdoor courts.

Educational demand has been encouraged by the development of short tennis but the poor state of LEA tennis courts in the authority is a real disincentive to promote the game. The potential for tennis amongst school children is considerable, requiring the active support of a Tennis Development Officer. The ITI proposal would be a welcomed extension to school work, but the cost of transporting pupils would probably be prohibitive.

The Newcastle Parks Tennis Scheme has been organised since 1983 and takes advantage of outdoor courts in a variety of venues. The objectives of the scheme are compatible with the Leisure Services commitment to participation at all levels. More young people playing tennis could use an indoor facility for winter work. In 1988 some 600 or so registered players attended.

Private club members' demand might come from the 3,000 club members in LTA affiliated clubs in Northumberland. Once a centre becomes a likely prospect, players outside the normal catchment area might well be encouraged into travelling. A survey of club members would prove valuable particularly in response to prospects for winter participation and the pay-as-you-play arrangement.

In summary, managers must quantify the demographic, economic and social variables. The known sources of information must be pursued and organised tennis clubs and groups should be surveyed.

Building and siting options
The LTA can advise on low cost permanent structures with ancillary accommodation. It can also recommend surfaces and contractors for indoor courts. At 1989 prices a figure near 700,000 would be suited to one of the proposed facilities but local decisions should be made concerning the environmental impact of the design structure.

A number of access points need to be identified. Sub-surface research is also necessary, although early studies indicated there were no major problems. Existing tennis facilities at Paddy Freemans comprised 12 disused derelict courts. The cost of resurfacing and developing a club plus an ITI facility would therefore not be as expensive as starting from scratch. Resurfacing costs were approximately 20,000 for three outdoor courts using all weather macadam.

Planning permission
Apart from obvious requirements including visual landscaping, design characteristics and access arrangements, there appeared to be every prospect of

success in gaining planning permission for an ITI at Paddy Freemans. With the City Council cooperating and acting as a partner to the scheme it would be an added advantage in seeking planning permission.

Neighbourhood support for the development is always advantageous, particularly at the planning approval stage.

Financial viability

Even in so straightforward a case it is clear that a lot of work had to be done by the appropriate managers. It would take time to pull all the data together and prepare a report. Even with the work contracted to consultants there is a cost in the money and time spent preparing a feasibility study.

The financial burden of preparing an argument will always be less than the cost of operating a major sports and recreation facility. Just as it is important for the feasibility study to make some accurate judgements, so it is vital that financial projections on a longer timescale are based on likely outcome and not on an imagined scenario.

Earlier figures indicate that development costs would be 700,000 – 750,000 with the LTA prepared to offer 33 per cent grant aid.

The City Council had real difficulties in offering financial assistance but with the Council owning the site it was argued that providing the land would make a significant contribution.

In terms of operational financing, management needed to decide on a pricing structure that reflected likely demand at peak and off peak times. Differences in demand between winter and summer also had to be built into the pricing policy.

One aspect of the research phase needed to discover the usage rates of other similar centres and to calculate, on the basis of local knowledge, the best and worst case scenarios. Summer usage of 40 per cent and winter usage of 80 per cent to 90 per cent (off peak and peak times) would provide some guidance towards income targets.

Pricing policies in Newcastle-Upon-Tyne would be fairly difficult. Paddy Freemans is adjacent to an area that is essentially middle class but the city's policy is to encourage participation in all groups. Preferential treatment towards target groups would almost certainly involve the city in negotiations with future management.

Lawn Tennis Association recommended, or locally determined, staff levels, income and total expenditure forecasts must be detailed before reaching the decision to proceed. Producing data is perhaps inappropriate in these few pages since local conditions, trends, social and economic profiles will influence the first financial projections. A financial costing on Paddy Freemans, it is suggested, should lead to a small operating profit. Although the capital investment and land value were not included in expenditure figures they should be taken into account by senior managers in this kind of exercise.

At a time when all managers are having to examine costs, justify one service against another and make spending cuts if necessary, the provision of a new resource will require careful consideration. Ultimately decisions will be based on cost and on the contribution a scheme makes to organisational objectives.

This discussion does not seek to present one viable ITI centre as an example for others to follow. For those involved in the development of sport, and in facility management, the tennis case study has provided an opportunity to consider many of the key points, particularly the need for cooperation, coordination and partnerships are recurring themes. Planning ahead, obtaining all required information, monitoring progress and determining review procedures are essential to all those in sports and facility development.

The LTA's willingness to invest in local schemes is most encouraging and one hopes our stock of indoor tennis facilities will continue to improve.

Figure 6.2 Indoor tennis initiative: an action schedule

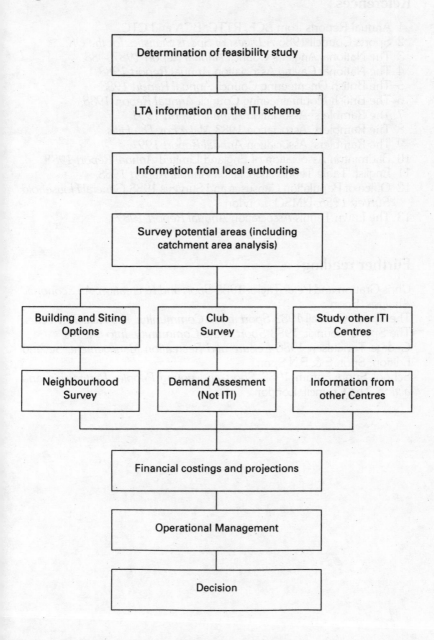

The review process is ongoing.

References

1 Annual Reports from BCF, RTTC, BCA and CTC.
2 Sports Council 1986 *A Digest of Sports Statistics for the UK.*
3 The National Angler's Council *Annual Report 1987 – 88.*
4 The National Caving Association *Annual Report 1988.*
5 The British Orienteering Council *Annual Report 1988.*
6 The British Mountaineering Council *Annual Report 1988.*
7 The Ramblers' Association *Annual Report 1991.*
8 The Ramblers' Association 1983 *Make For The Hills.*
9 The Ramblers' Association *Annual Report 1991.*
10 Badminton Association of England Limited *Annual Report 1988.*
11 English Table Tennis Association *Annual Report 1988.*
12 Office of Population Censuses and Surveys 1988 *General Household Survey 1986.* HMSO, London.
13 The Lawn Tennis Association *Annual Report 1987*

Further reading

Chris Gratton and Peter Taylor 1985 *Sport and Recreation: An Economic Analysis.* Spon.
The Sports Council 1982 *Sport in the Community: The Next Ten Years.*
The Sports Council, 1988 *Sport in the Community, Into the 90s.*
George Torkildsen 1986 *Leisure and Recreation Management.* Second Edition, Spon/E & F N Spon.
School Sport Forum 1988 *Sport and young People: Partnership and action.* The Council, London.

7 A case for sport

Case Study: Novocastrians Rugby Union Football Club, Newcastle-upon-Tyne

This case study brings together many of those organisations involved, in one way or another, with the promotion of sport. It is a story of how one junior sports club found itself facing the possible loss of grounds and club facilities. In one way or another the following organisations have an influence, direct or indirect, upon the outcome:

1. Department of the Environment
2. The Sports Council (National and Regional)
3. The Central Council for Physical Recreation
4. The National Playing Fields Association
5. The Institute of Leisure and Amenity Management
6. The Rugby Football Union
7. Newcastle-upon-Tyne Metropolitan Borough Council
8. Newcastle Sports Council
9. A developer
10. Novocastrians Rugby Union Football Club (Members and friends) and
11. The Royal Grammar School, Newcastle-upon-Tyne

The primary purpose of this section is to illustrate the role and contribution of various agencies or organisations in the fortunes of one sports club at a moment in time. To understand the relevance of a sports club in the North East of England to our appreciation of organisations and issues we must start with a consideration of sports planning criteria.

Planning for sport

Documents such as *Planning for Sport*, published in 1968,[1] have been superseded by a number of Sports Council publications leading up to the strategy, *Sport in the Community: Into the 90s*[2]. Proposals for the development of sport need to present planners with the information required concerning quantity, type and distribution. Local authorities having produced Unitary Development Plans (UDPs), Structure Plans or Local Plans, should by definition prepare sport or recreation plans as an integral component of these documents. Whilst documents produced at a national level can be useful, as guides to local action, there is a clear need for detailed local policies and plans based on real needs. Measures of inconsistency across Britain, both in the planning and provision of sport, effectively confirm that no successful method has yet been derived. Standards of provision for outdoor sports, swimming pools and sports centres do exist and they are used, but often for guidance purposes rather than for determining policy.

In 1991, and therefore following the determination of this case study, a Planning Policy Guide-line (PPG) 17: *Sport and Recreation* was issued jointly by the Department of the Environment and the Welsh Office[3]. The PPG 17 presents a strong case for the inclusion of organised sport and informal recreation in the preparation of development plans, indicating that land and water resources should be provided. Indeed the document makes it quite clear that the government attaches great importance to the retention of recreational and amenity open space in urban areas. In a positive commitment to open space, PPG 17 also sets out a presumption against inappropriate development of the green belt, although provision for outdoor sport is seen as one of the most appropriate uses. It is further recommended that playing fields be normally protected except where:

- sports and recreation facilities can best be retained and enhanced through the redevelopment of a small part of the site
- alternative provision of equivalent community benefit is made available
- the local plan shows an excess of sports pitch provision and public open space in the area, taking account of the recreation and amenity value of such provision

The PPG 17 also states that local plans should include a statement on community need for sports pitches, on policies for the protection of playing fields and a regard for the Register of Recreational Land as prepared by the Sports Council (with the CCPR and the NPFA).

The National Playing Fields Association (NPFA) continues to offer six acres of open space as the requirement for a 1000 population.[4] Local authorities, with a planning responsibility, can and do look at NPFA standards, but they are not required to adopt them. Local circumstances should encourage recreation and planning departments to devise their own standards, particularly when nationally derived figures may not be valid or take note of local requirements. However a systematic approach to determining open space requirements remains, for many local authorities, an intellectual rather than a pragmatic exercise.

Providing for outdoor sport in Newcastle

The local authority sees itself complementing the voluntary sector and recognises that participation has increased dramatically since the mid 1960s. Local experience suggests a continuing trend of increased participation in traditional sports and a favourable public response to new sports. It is recognised, however, that current activities favour male participation.

Of direct relevance to this case study is the locally recognised minimum standard of 1.1 hectares (2.7 acres) of outdoor sports provision in the city, per 1000 residents. (This compares with 1.6-1.8 hectares, or 4-4.5 acres, in the NPFA targets for provision). Local circumstances determine a lower figure for Newcastle-upon-Tyne. Targets need to be realisable if they are to have any meaning. Existing public playing field provision in the city amounts to only 0.47 hectares per 1000 residents, which, even when added to dual use school and further education facilities, come to only 0.73 hectares. Clearly, even by its own standards, there is a deficiency of playing fields in Newcastle. This deficiency, apart from the northern parts of the city, is spread across the built up area.

Novocastrians RUFC

Formed in 1899 by the old boys of the Royal Grammar School (RGS) the club became known as Old Novocastrians RFC. In 1926/27 the club moved to Sutherland Park then owned by B J Sutherland and Co but purchased by the RGS in 1939. The sports fields at Sutherland Park occupy approximately 13.36 hectares and include three rugby pitches, a clubhouse, a caretaker's house, a cricket square and six tarmac tennis courts.

The rugby club opened in 1969, since which time its playing fortunes improved. Novocastrians is one of three open rugby clubs in the city of Newcastle, the others being (Newcastle) Gosforth RFC and Northern RFC. All three clubs run seven senior sides. Newcastle University and Medicals RFC also run a number of sides, although they are not open to the general public. The Polytechnic (now the University of Northumbria) only runs sides on a Wednesday with students playing for club sides on Saturdays.

Pupils of the RGS are specifically proposed as honorary members of the club and close personal links have always been maintained by the school and the club. Current membership of the club stands at approximately 250, including about 60 old boys of the RGS.

The rugby club and the school both used the sports facilities for nearly 60 years until the school effectively had little further need for them in 1984. Novocastrians had enjoyed a favourable relationship with the school which, as owner of the land made a charge for the use of facilities.

The Royal Grammar School, having no continuing need for the facilities, applied for outline planning permission in 1986. The planning application sought outline consent for the erection of residential development on the school's sports facilities at Sutherland Park. Following a Development Control Sub Committee meeting in 1986 (of the City Council) it was resolved that permission be refused for the following reason:

> In the opinion of the City Council as District Planning Authority the proposed development would result in a significant loss of recreational facilities in a part of the city which is already suffering from a substantial deficiency in playing field provision to the detriment of the amenity of residents in this part of the city (May 1986).[5]

Refusal was based on the loss of recreational land and not on the basis of housing.

From the school's point of view there was good enough reason to seek a realisation of its asset. With the value of land clearly related to its development potential, housing offered a much more attractive proposition than selling it for prevailing sports use. The facilities continued to cost the school money and prospects for the future confirmed it had no further use of the fields. Indeed, money was required to enhance, or repair, the sports facilities at the school.

The appeal

It was on this basis that the RGS appealed to the Secretary of State at the Department of the Environment. Essentially the appeal was against the decision of the City Council to refuse planning permission.

The rugby club, threatened by an uncertain future, was forced to support the city. This actually required a significant amount of work for a small volunteer organisation. Support and advice were required from a number of sources and for different reasons.

In considering the risk to its future, Novocastrians looked at:

- preparing a bid for Sutherland Park
- buying or leasing alternative facilities
- sharing a sports ground
- fighting the appeal in a professional manner

A bid to purchase Sutherland Park, with an appeal pending, was not attractive to the owners. With outline permission for housing the value of the land could be increased six- or seven-fold.

Sharing a sports ground had to be considered seriously, given the threat to their own viability. The exercise was easily completed. There were no organisations in the public or private sectors who had the ability to share a facility. Either there were no facilities available or existing playing fields were already extensively used.

Buying or leasing an alternative facility required the identification of a potential site, a feasibility exercise on its viability and the preparation of a financial package. It is essential that any sports club should determine if financial support may be forthcoming from:

- the local authority
- the Regional Sports Council
- club membership
- a brewery and other sponsors

Here the exercise assumed an added complexity. Emotions ran high over the possible loss of the existing facilities. Support for purchasing Sutherland Park would have attracted assistance from many older members, both previous pupils of the school and former players, but any move to an alternative facility would have proved a less exciting prospect. Quite apart from any emotional element, the effect any move would have on membership would be difficult to determine.

Contesting an appeal of this nature requires careful preparation; it also demands an element of confidentiality. Members of any club would find difficulty in protecting information used in evidence at an appeal. This actually complicates the consideration of alternative facilities since few should even be aware of the option. Clearly a recreational asset is less likely to be retained if the club, and in Novocastrians' case its seven teams, were to reappear at new facilities.

It may seem a hard economic fact of life but whenever available land was identified it was nearly always targeted 'for development purposes'. Only on one occasion did sports fields, protected by a trust, become available. Despite fairly rapid organisation it proved difficult for a voluntary body to move as quickly as a commercial concern or a local authority. Financial packages involving loans, grant aid and donations take time to pull together. In this case Proctor and Gamble sold its playing fields and club facilities to North Tyneside MBC.

In examining the four options, three were effectively ruled out. The school would not sell at playing field prices, it had a far better offer from a major developer; no other fields were available and no one had the capacity to share.

Joining hands with the local authority, and presenting a professional challenge to the appeal was always the most likely prospect. What was less certain was the outcome. Over recent years there have been a number of planning applications to develop sports fields. The interest and the efforts of the CCPR and the NPFA have already been noted in this regard.

There are times when local authorities will refuse planning permission with the justification based on the local structure plans. Alternatively a scheme which seems progressive and likely to contribute to the quality of life could well receive encouragement. Although local policies will guide decision making, there are few hard and fast rules which govern all applications. This case study considers the arguments that sought to persuade the inspector at appeal that the Appellant's case was not acceptable. Any organisation undergoing a similar experience will require a considerable amount of negotiation, planning and organising if it is to present its case effectively.

Not all planning appeals are fought on the same basis. Loss of recreational land can occur for a number of reasons, ranging from: fields that have not been used for some seasons, clubs who have found alternative premises and industrial concerns or commercial organisations which can no longer afford their upkeep. Clearly much also depends on the club or team using a facility and how it sees the future. At a political and economic level local authorities can find themselves under some difficult pressures. For example, if a company wanted to extend by building on its own playing fields, in order to develop business and recruit additional employees, the pressure would be considerable. Even if there was a 'sitting tenant' in the shape of a sports club, the risk of losing a major employer is an unenviable prospect for any chief executive or council leader.

In the case of Novocastrians RUFC a strategy was prepared on both broad and narrow fronts. The city was to defend its earlier decision and could call on experienced planners and recreationists to give evidence. The club itself could examine the specific case for its sport, in this case rugby union, and consider in detail the prospects for both winning and losing the appeal.

From the political point of view there are a number of organisations at national, regional and local level who need to be informed. Some will offer advice, others may be able to offer direct support.

1   At a local level the following could well have a role:
    – local residents and their Community Association
    – local schools who supply players to the club
    – the local Sports Council (voluntary organisation)
    – similar sports clubs within a defined catchment area
    – the local authority itself, through an appropriate officer

2　At a regional level the Sports Council should be informed and its support enlisted. Providing it is familiar with the circumstances the view of professional peers needs to be recognised. The appropriate constituent body of the sport should be able to confirm the club's status.

3　Nationally there are a few organisations who will offer encouragement and support. It is most likely that the Sports Council will refer to regional offices but the CCPR and the NPFA will provide advice. The governing body itself should be kept informed as indeed might your local Member of Parliament. Every pressure should be brought to bear.

Any sports organisation seeking to convince an inspector of its continuing viability might wish to consider alternative financial strategies. 'What if' scenarios, costed out and clearly thought through, are likely to have some impact. Essentially the sports club needed to persuade the inspector that the loss of grounds would have a detrimental effect on rugby and sport in general in Newcastle.

From a practical point of view it would be necessary to write to the inspector, independent of the local authority, requesting to give evidence. Where the local authority figures may not give due emphasis to an argument, this should be explored. What latent demand exists for the sport, has another club been in a similar position and what are local community needs? Where similar appeals have been heard the results can be useful. The Institute of Leisure and Amenity Management offers a number of services to members including the facility to exchange ideas and problems. The emphasis here has been on a junior sports club's relationship to a planning appeal. There is no doubt however that the local authority plays an instrumental role in this exercise. Without the strong support of Newcastle-upon-Tyne Planning and Leisure Services Departments, this case might have had a different complexion.

The relevant act concerning this kind of planning appeal is the Town and Country Planning Act 1971, Section 36 and schedule 9.[6]

New and substantially improved powers to enforce planning control have subsequently been given to local planning authorities by the Planning and Compensation Act 1991, and explained in the PPG 18: *Enforcing Planning Control*.

Conclusion

The Inspector at a planning appeal represents the Secretary of State for the Department of the Environment. Ultimately he or she advises the Secretary of State on a preferred outcome to the appeal. It is for the Secretary of State to make the decision. The Inspector's report considered the views of the Appellant, the local authority and the rugby club and concluded:

Point 11　The present and long-standing use of the appeal site in planning terms is that of a sports ground and the permanent loss of the three pitches should be seen primarily in the context of playing field provision generally in the city. The council has taken the basic playing field standards as variously advised by the Sports Council and the National Playing Fields Association and applied them to the local conditions obtaining in Newcastle. The provision which it aims for is 1.1 hectares per 1,000 population and it was not contended at the inquiry that this standard was unreasonable. Compared with this standard the present overall provision in the city (including detached school playing fields) is 0.6 hectares per 1,000 population which is about 57 per cent of the target figure. In the east of the city, where the appeal site lies, the provision is not significantly different. Faced with this substantial shortfall the council is making considerable efforts both to provide additional pitches and (also on the basis that pitch quality has a considerable bearing on the level of participation in outdoor games) to improve existing pitches. Against this background, I consider that the loss of three pitches, one of excellent and two of reasonable quality, would be serious. The pitches are of course presently used for the playing of rugby and whilst the present deficiency in the perceived need for rugby pitches (18 pitches available out of 19 pitches required) is not nearly as serious as that for other sports, I have no doubt that the loss of three out of the existing 18 pitches would have severe consequences for the playing of the game in the city. I have concluded therefore, bearing in mind the present deficiency in playing field provision within the city, the quality of the pitches at Sutherland Park and the number of pitches needed for playing rugby in the city as a whole, that the loss of the pitches contained within the appeal site would be a serious blow to the playing of outdoor sport within the city.

Point 12   The Appellants say that as the club is a private one, access to the facilities is not available to members of the public as of right and that consequently the club's three pitches should not be included within those available for members of the public. I find this argument unconvincing. It is true that members of the public cannot simply turn up at Sutherland Park and play rugby (or other games) as of right. They first have to join the club. This is equally true of the other two rugby union clubs in the city (Newcastle) Gosforth and Northern and on this argument those pitches should also be excluded from the figure for available pitches. Even the pitches owned by the city council would not pass the test of user, as of right, as the consent of that body has first to be obtained before use. I do not consider therefore that this is a realistic approach as it ignores the realities of the playing of rugby within the city.

Point 15   Faced with a situation where the only authorised use is that of a sports ground, the school, if it retains ownership, will probably wish to derive whatever financial benefit it can from the ground. This means using or permitting the use for recreational purposes and, in a situation where use by the school has declined over the years and has now ceased, this use is not likely to be primarily associated with the school. It is more likely in my view that the land will continue to be used as a sports ground probably for the playing of rugby. If the ground is sold to a developer as a long-term investment, the new owner will in all likelihood wish to make something of the investment in the meantime; the ground is unlikely to be left fallow. In these circumstances I think it likely that the use as a sports ground will continue probably for the playing of rugby. Bearing these matters in mind I am satisfied, on the balance of probabilities, that if permission for the present proposal is refused, Sutherland Park will continue to be used for outdoor sport, most probably for the playing of rugby, for the foreseeable future.

Point 16   I have so far confined myself to considering the effect of the proposal in terms of loss of pitches which in my view is serious enough to warrant refusal of permission. However it would be wrong to ignore in this case the effect on the Novocastrians of the loss of their long-standing home and the consequent effect on the playing of rugby in the city. I heard at the inquiry that in Newcastle, as in many other areas, the playing of rugby union (outside schools and other educational establishments) is associated almost exclusively with the three clubs within the city. As one of those three clubs, the Novocastrians make a substantial contribution to the playing of the game within the city. In these circumstances the effect on the club is a matter I am entitled to take into account in coming to my decision. In this connection I accept the evidence of the club that if Sutherland Park is lost to it there are no available sports facilities to which the club could transfer and that consequently it would appear the club would fail. If the appeal is dismissed however there appears to be at least a fair possibility that the club will continue for the foreseeable future at Sutherland Park. For these reasons also I consider that the proposal would have serious consequences for the playing of outdoor sport within the city.

I have to say that in the final analysis I do not regard these benefits as outweighing the loss to the city of these playing fields and the contribution they make and can continue to make to the playing of outdoor sport.
Reference Application No.: NC/OUT/01/38/86[7]

Voluntary organisations are the backbone of British sport but they remain self-determining organisations. Their ability to promote sport and develop excellence is keenly influenced by their financial viability. Until a way is found to equip the voluntary sector with the appropriate skills and necessary resources for self management there will be problems, even casualties. Clearly the defence or enhancement of our sporting culture currently leaves much to the determination of a few. It can be of little wonder that those best placed to protect themselves are the most likely to survive. One certain way forward is the need to establish partnerships both within governing bodies and between compatible organisations including local authorities. In this way clubs and local organisations can prepare their own development strategies, consider and include the needs of their community, the disadvantaged groups and those with special needs. Where Novocastrians survived others may perish.

This case study presents an argument for protecting specific playing fields. The reader should now refer to the earlier section on the NPFA and prepare a note of the methods used in contesting any planning application which threatens open space used for sport and recreation.

References

1 The Sports Council 1968 *Planning for Sport.*
2 The Sports Council 1988 *Sport in the Community, Into the 90s.*
3 The Department of the Environment 1991 *Planning Policy Guide-line, Sport and Recreation.* HMSO, London.
4 The National Playing Fields Association 1986 *Outdoor Playing Space Requirements, 6 Act Target.* NPFA, London.
5 Newcastle-Upon-Tyne MBC May 1986 Minutes of Development Control Sub-Committee (Unpublished).
6 Town and Country Planning Act 1971, Section 36 and schedule 9, HMSO, London.
7 Department of Environment, 1987, Result of Planning Appeal, Local Authority Ref. NC/OUT/01/38/86, DOE, London (Unpublished).

8 The commercial sector

The significant changes that have taken place in leisure and the service sector represent an important feature of the developing economic structure of the UK. Local authorities, commercial and voluntary organisations all contribute to a dynamic environment where sport and physical recreation form just a part of a diverse leisure industry. It would be mistaken to discount the nature of the relationship between these sectors. The survival of many voluntary organisations, particularly sports clubs, can depend on the contribution made by bar profits. There can be interesting partnerships between commercial organisations and sport bodies. Sponsorship of sport has played an increasingly important role in sports development. Professional sportsmen and women are either salaried or they compete for prize money. There are even amateur sports which have determined that payments may be made to performers. Recent interest in the development of sport on television could well afford new opportunities for growth to a number of activities. Television coverage encouraged the sports of snooker, darts, athletics and football as popular pastimes. Leisure industries have diversified into wide-ranging profit-seeking organisations that not only offer sport and recreation but also focus on gambling, packages for tourists, night clubs and discos, theatres, cinemas, public houses, caravan parks and so on.

Commercial organisations have diversified into, or away from, sport and recreation in order that they can maximise sales, and increase market share to achieve growth. There may be an interest in the sporting programme but the commercial company cannot be motivated just by a love of sport. The profit motive must be central to their purpose. This does not mean that they cannot offer similar activities to those owned and managed by the public sector and by voluntary organisations. Squash, tennis and badminton are offered by the three types of organisation (public, private for profit, and private not for profit) and as such these facilities would be seen as in competition with each other.

At the same time the leisure sector is largely a fragmented industry with mergers and take overs confirming the diversity of interests. Prospects for 1993 and beyond, with a single European market, must interest many organisations on both sides of the Channel. There is now every prospect for European companies in merging, taking over, or competing for business in all member nations. A European network of business interests appears attractive, particularly at a time when new, larger markets are about to open up.

Industrial provision

One further supplier of facilities and opportunities is the industrial concern providing for employees as a fringe benefit. The advantages of a fit workforce are recognised in other economies, particularly in the USA and Japan, more than in the UK, but there are signs that this may change as the benefits are more fully recognised.

These industrial sports clubs in the UK developed through the late nineteenth and early twentieth centuries. Reasons for their growth varied from employer concern for worker welfare to a determination to encourage loyalty to the firm. The 1960s, however, witnessed a considerable decline in provision as employers sought to redefine their role and relationship with employees. During the 1970s, 1980s and early 1990s the loss of playing fields and sports facilities owned by companies has also been significant. There are always exceptions to the rule as demonstrated by Nissan UK, based in Sunderland, where the company have recently provided well appointed indoor sports facilities and a floodlight pitch for the benefit of employees. Some companies are also beginning to take an interest in corporate fitness programmes, working with either the local university or a commercial leisure club for monitoring and assessment.

Compulsory competitive tendering

The introduction of compulsory competitive tendering is most likely to witness an increased number of commercial companies, from inside and outside the leisure sector, tendering for and winning contracts to manage publicly owned sport and recreation facilities. The relationship between public and private sectors therefore should develop significantly. Public and commercial organisations will also be required to manage according to social and financial objectives. The satisfaction of social objectives will present a challenge to the commercial sector while the public sector must adopt a pragmatic response to financial targets if it is to compete for and win contracts. Certainly partnerships will be formed that go beyond sports sponsorship contracts. The commercial sector currently lacks the skilled management personnel to take full advantage of CCT. Career prospects for effective public sector managers might, in response to this, look very interesting indeed.

Sponsorship

It has been estimated that sport sponsorship has risen from 129 million in 1985 to 226 million in 1990.[1] Sponsorship has been dominated by a few televised sports. Horse racing remains an important industry in this respect. However, television has provided a rather uncertain partner for sport. Contracts between national governing bodies, a television company and the sponsor must seek to recognise that each partner has to satisfy what may be contrasting objectives. Satellite television has introduced more competition into the broadcasting of sport with some events of national interest being won by satellite corporations at the expense of the more traditional television companies. Governing bodies will seek to maintain their control over a sport but pressures will undoubtedly arise to assuage either the television company or the sponsors.

Examples of commercial activity

With such diversity of organisational interest and design a consideration of special features from a few commercial organisations will illustrate the current situation. Although the early 1990s have witnessed an economic recession, ending a period of some ten years of growth in the leisure sector, consumer expenditure on leisure is still estimated to be 74 billion in 1989. This figure represents approximately 23 per cent of total consumer expenditure. The Henley Centre has estimated that 9.75 billion is spent on sport and related goods and services. Although gambling, estimated at 2.84 billion, makes up an important element in this figure it is significant that sports participation accounts for some 1.61 billion. The largest sport market for clothing, footwear and equipment is golf which the Centre for Leisure Research[2] estimated at 250 million in 1990 with Keep fit/aerobics the second highest at 173 million.

Skiing is another big and competitive business, attracting one-fifth of the European holiday market. Ski packages to Europe have largely been standardised in order to attract an improved market share. Large organisations, including some who have diversified into leisure, recognise that most ski holiday packages are bought by customers who are repeat skiers. Tour operators faced by keen competition can therefore be expected to seek new resorts with centres that offer more winter activities, like cross country skiing, and better access arrangements.

The privatisation of water will also place ownership of recreational amenity in the hands of companies where financial objectives are paramount. There seems little doubt that a private organisation will seek to maximise its profits. Access and facility provision, for sport and recreation, on or around our major inland water areas could be seen as another business opportunity. Charging individuals for access to areas of outstanding beauty, or for providing sporting amenity, is no longer a far fetched concept.

In 1988 there were only 34 indoor bowling facilities, 17 of them owned by AMF. Over the following few years bowling became as growth area with perhaps as many as 90 or 100 new centres planned. Although they can cost over 2 million to build, the financial returns can be attractive. In the mid 1990s the fashionable area of high technology games seems to be headed towards what has been described as games of virtual reality. The market has become both diverse and dynamic and it is therefore important for all organisations in sport and recreation to appreciate what is actually attracting people to spend their leisure time and money.

The key to success is still likely to be an emphasis on entertainment. Although profits are being maintained, squash and snooker appears to have reached something of a plateau with little or no growth. Indeed the relative decline in television coverage may have had an effect on participation figures. Some facilities once used as snooker halls have been converted to accommodate the new interest in laser shoot outs and high technology entertainment.

Support funding for sport

With reference often made to the lack of finance for sport and the problems faced by the voluntary sector in particular it is encouraging that two schemes have been introduced which should have a really positive impact. In 1991 The Foundation for Sport and the Arts was launched with a fund of some 60 million a year; 40 million available for sport and 20 million for the arts. The money has been provided by the pools promoters and by a reduction in the Pool Betting Duty. Early beneficiaries were the Sports Aid Foundation and the National Coaching Foundation, each of which received a significant grant. The Trustees are prepared to consider applications for grant aid that focus on training schemes, regional and local facilities, equipment for clubs, schemes that focus on young people, sport for people with a disability, sports medicine and funds for major competition. It is important that applications focus on athletic sport; adventure play equipment may be included. Whilst the 40 million per year for sport is extremely welcome it is apparent that the 500 applications a week reaching the Foundation are stretching the administration somewhat. It is also evident that the Trustees do not appear to have a strategy, based on need, for allocating the money other than those stated in their policy guide-lines. The regional offices of the Sports Council have the strategies, have identified the needs and highlighted priorities but have limited funding. Nevertheless the availability of significant moneys must be welcomed; it is certainly appreciated that much of the money will go to community based or grass roots initiatives. It is unfortunate however that the decision to award a grant appears to be arbitrary and that there has been a backlog of applications from the beginning; due it seems to the small staffing complement at the Foundation.

Sportsmatch is a second new source of money, worth 3 million a year of government money, providing individual schemes offer matched funding from business sponsors. The scheme was first announced in the Minister of

Sport's Review 'Sport and Active Recreation' in 1991 and was introduced in late 1992. The scheme is administered by the Institute of Sports Sponsorship, the Scottish Sports Council and the Sports Council for Wales. Of course it would be equally appropriate to profile this scheme in the chapter on central government but the most interesting and challenging dimension to obtaining a Sportsmatch grant is the ability to obtain business sponsorship. Applications need to have at least 1000 of new sponsorship (500 in Wales) for a sports event of some description. Government moneys would then match the business sponsorship up to 75,000 per annum. The scheme represents an excellent encouragement to clubs and organisations. Perhaps the problem might be the availability of new business money during a recession, the promotional skills required to attract sponsorship and the ability to present a persuasive case. Taken together and with the prospect of a National Lottery, sport should benefit enormously from the injection of much needed money.

Summary of key points

1 British sport contains a fascinating mix of organisations with motives that range from the pursuit of excellence to the maximisation of profits. Professional football and horse racing are two sports which appear to be profit oriented. Whether they achieve profits or not will not necessarily be determined by similar variables.
2 It should be remembered that although texts can discuss public and private sectors, voluntary and commercial organisations, there is a relationship and an interdependence between many of these organisations. Ultimate objectives may not be quite the same but the means to achieve various ends are not so dissimilar.
3 British sport offers a very rich mixture of organisations driven by political, economic and social objects. The determination of success will vary, but few can ignore financial viability as an essential goal, particularly in the commercial sector.
4 During the 1990s the face of commercial sector sports amenity will be marked by development and diversification, and the ability of consumers to pay for services received. Although this may appear to be little different from the 1980s, some of the activity will be based in areas where management was previously public and objectives were social rather than economic.

     The following section profiles two organisations in the Commercial sector; one which focuses on health and fitness and one highlights an industrial organisation providing sport and recreation opportunities for employees.

Case study: Apex Fitness Systems Ltd

Success in the private sector depends on the ability to identify an opportunity for facility or programme development and to deliver a service which offers quality and value in an atmosphere of customer care. This ambition should be no different to those managing the voluntary or public sector organisations although the price of failure is perhaps measured in different terms if your livelihood depends on it.

It is in this context that this case study profiles one commercial sector organisation and the success of a business man who appreciated an opportunity when he saw one and had the necessary vision to develop a number of projects into profitable and viable concerns. Mr Charles Buchanan first started his involvement with owning and managing leisure clubs when he opened Ivy Court Leisure Club, Newcastle-Upon-Tyne, in 1982. In the ten years that followed he established a further seven leisure clubs and an equipment division which supplies fitness centres and leisure clubs across the UK and Ireland.

Apex Fitness Systems Ltd controls two distinct business activities; both are directed by the owner. One, Ivy Court Leisure Clubs, focuses on the acquisition and operation of leisure facilities while the second acts as the UK distributor for STAR TRAC Treadmills, an American range of fitness equipment. Two Ivy Court Leisure Clubs are based in both Newcastle-Upon-Tyne and Durham, while there is one each in Whitley Bay, Sunderland, Glasgow and Edinburgh. The five star Sheraton Hotel in Edinburgh is targeted towards a particular market segment, while the two clubs in Durham operate from local authority facilities and are geared to a community focused market. The remaining five clubs operate in the more traditional fashion of commercial facilities based in urban areas with significant populations.

The addition of new facilities to the Ivy Court Leisure Clubs came as a result of a successful track record and business opportunism. The Sheraton Hotel sought advice from Mr Buchanan following the disappointing performance of their leisure club and at a time when they only had 70 members. Ivy Court Leisure Clubs took over and restored the business within a two year period. Since 1990 the membership has risen to 750 people. The City of Durham wanted to create a quality fitness amenity within two community based sports centres but did not want the risk of investing in expensive equipment and lacked some of the experience in this specific aspect of the leisure market. Further centres acquired in Newcastle-Upon-Tyne, Whitley Bay and Glasgow came when opportunities arose. Invariably they received major refurbishment, including new equipment designed to be popular with the club members.

The Equipment Division operates from the north east of England and London, plus Ireland under an agency agreement. A sales manager, service manager and contract engineer provide the necessary support to over 300 clubs (and private facilities) which use STAR TRAC equipment. The division provides cover for the period equipment is under guarantee and subsequently to service agreements. The distribution rights to STAR TRAC are based on achieving a minimum of sales each year and satisfying quality after-sales standards.

To fully understand the nature and extent of the success of Apex Fitness Systems Ltd one needs to look beyond the energy and opportunism of one individual within the business community and examine the shrewd judgements and management skills that are necessary to ensure longer term success. Basic features of business success such as providing customer care, a quality environment, the use of 'motivational' (user friendly) equipment, well trained and motivated staff, a diverse social programme and a commitment to high standards are all important aspects of the Ivy Court Leisure Club operation.

Club membership

There are few secrets to some of the decisions that must be taken when determining the feasibility of a project; particularly a leisure club. The commercial viability of a leisure club operation normally requires a catchment area population of approximately 100,000 within a three mile radius. The desired membership levels are variable and dependent upon the market the club serves but a two per cent minimum, or 2,000 people, should make a business profitable. Achieving more than two per cent needs to be sustained with the recognition that leisure clubs can often lose between 50 and 75 per cent of their membership each year.

Membership figures for the Ivy Court clubs in 1993 ranged from 750 at the Sheraton Hotel in Edinburgh, to 1,500 at one of the clubs in Newcastle-Upon Tyne, 2,000 at Whitley Bay and 3,000 in Glasgow. Total membership amounts to some 10,000 people across the eight clubs.

The record of membership renewals at the Ivy Court Clubs is nearer 75 per cent. With annual membership within the division running at 200 to 500, including a joining fee and depending on the club and its location it is clearly important to retain members from one year to the next. Only one class of member exists and a single tariff membership scheme operates at all eight clubs. The membership profile of all eight clubs recognises that the average age is likely to be near 40 years and 65 per cent of members will be female. Alcohol and food are not sold in the clubs in the belief that it would detract from a concentration on providing a quality service.

Management of leisure club operations

Each club has two duty managers responsible for membership, sales and operational aspects. In addition the leisure club division employs reception staff, fitness consultants, a training manager, an aerobics coordinator, a general manager and professional support in accounts and legal aspects. In total the division employs about 80 staff to operate the eight clubs.

Quality control

To ensure continued customer satisfaction there are clear guide-lines concerning customer care. The motto of 'cleanliness and friendliness' is very much a part of the Ivy Court attitude towards club management.

Controlling staff costs is as important in the leisure sector as any other business community and as the following model suggests the Ivy Court clubs seek to confine staff costs within 27.5 per cent of turnover.

A typical centre might be based on the following projections:

Catchment area	100,000 people
Membership (2 per cent of population)	2,000 people
Membership income @ 250 p.a.	500,000
Equipment lease	50,000
Staff costs (at 27.5 per cent of membership fees only)	137,500
Operational costs (Inclusive of central costs)	263,000
Profit	50,000

These approximate figures do illustrate the need for tight financial control. Indeed it could mean the difference between a reasonable profit of 10 per cent, 50,000, or a loss of a similar amount. The Ivy Court clubs do not sell alcohol or food and as such the generation of additional income is limited. The danger of over investment in equipment and committing too much of the cash flow to capital costs can be overcome by lease or hire purchase agreements. Even the latest fitness equipment in this market becomes obsolete within a three to five year period and with a club requiring some 150,000 of investment.

The two divisions of Apex Fitness Systems Ltd have a turnover of approximately 3 million per annum.

Case Study: Sellafield Area Sports and Recreation Association

Industrial sector management of facilities

British Nuclear Fuels Limited (BNFL) operates as a commercial organisation. Profits are sought in the nuclear fuel industry but the need to have a motivated and contented work force has led to investment in the provision of sport and recreation services.

Employees at Sellafield, in Cumbria, pay a small levy to the Sellafield Area Sports and Recreation Association (SASRA). In return benefits of membership include a fairly wide ranging sports, recreation and social programme in neighbouring communities.

The Falcon Complex, in Egremont, is a multi purpose facility that is used by a variety of sports sections[3]. It is located on a large site and membership is open to BNFL employees, associate members from the local community, family, retired and life members. The sports sections at the Falcon Complex include:

- Archery
- Cricket
- Hockey
- Judo
- Soccer and
- Squash

Some of these sports are seasonal while others enjoy the facilities throughout the year. Although SASRA has an executive committee and it employs staff to implement policies, the sections are largely managed by members. Volunteers assist the operation of sports clubs very much in the same way as any club in the voluntary sector. The apparent satisfaction with a delegated form of control can be and has been a source of conflict between different sections and between the executive and individual sections.

The sport sections are of varying size and strength. Squash has 360 members, soccer has 40 members, archery, judo and cricket have about 20 each and hockey about 30 members.

Although an independent organisation, SASRA relies on BNFL support to maintain services and standards. Resources are provided on the basis that employees benefit from well organised sport and recreation. The Falcon Complex in Egremont is used simply to provide an example of how tensions can arise in an industrial sports complex. In this case two broad difficulties have been experienced:

1. The diversity of members' interests can create problems for a multi purpose facility. Each section has needs which must be judged fairly by the executive. At the same time the relative strengths of various sections can present difficulties when establishing a hierarchy of need.
2. Like many sports clubs financial viability can be the result of the success of the social programme and bar facilities. As a conclusion to encouraging a social programme and associate members it is possible for an organisation to lose the necessary balance between social and recreational objectives.

BNFL, like any other industrial provider, has to consider a third issue. What is the actual and potential involvement of SASRA members that makes their investment worthwhile? It is important, even in a major industry, for a commercial organisation to judge the social objectives and achievements against the financial support a sports and recreation programme enjoys. This integration of purpose should be present in both the social and sporting dimensions of the Falcon Complex.

This example highlights a dilemma for one sports executive and its paid officers. Although SASRA makes an effective contribution to the employees of BNFL the intention here is to explain the difficulties associated with a commercial organisation acting as benefactor, the elected committee and full-time officers managing a service, and the objectives of club members who have contrasting ambitions. Associate members, who by definition do not work for BNFL, and the full members who do, both have a perception of duty and customer care. With so much depending on the efforts of volunteers it is easy to see managers in the middle being pushed and pulled from both sides.

Underlying this difficulty there is also the embarrassment suffered by sections when they host visiting teams. It is custom and practice in many British sports for home teams to act as hosts once the game is over. The social contact enjoyed in the hour or so after competition has ended is an important part of the whole process. Visiting players and teams are shown a measure of hospitality which is returned at a later fixture. In order that sport sections can fulfil this obligation players and officials need to feel confident that facilities and services are made available. Without an encouraging atmosphere alternative provision, in local hotels and bars, may be considered. The willingness to fixture with a club can in part be a response to the total experience enjoyed between the two teams. The SASRA sections are no different in that they expect to honour their social obligations. It is also understandable that visitors identify the Falcon Complex and its sports teams with BNFL. Any disappointment they have with the facility can result in the company losing prestige.

The conclusion to this short case study focuses on the need for all commercial organisations, including industrial providers, to provide a meaningful coherent basis for management.

Organisations need to be proactive and not simply reactive. Objectives, social and sporting, must be identified and made known to all relevant parties. SASRA'S duty to its membership is to identify needs, provide opportunities and facilities and to review, on a regular basis, the success of its work.

Objectives may be declared on an annual basis but they should relate to a broader view as presented in an organisational strategy or plan. Reaching potential targets begins with a recognition that they can exist and that they are attainable.

Sport is an excellent medium through which to present a corporate image. SASRA, working as an extension to BNFL, needs to maximise its potential by encouraging the volunteers and sport sections into harmonious and cooperative effort. The SASRA employed recreation officers need to develop good communications between all relevant parts of the organisation. It is through effective working links that individuals or groups can prepare and develop plans, identify objectives and work with common purpose towards coherent goals.

Perhaps the underlying principle in this case study is the same for any manager in the public or private sector. A commitment to growth is essential if an organisation is to stand any chance of achieving corporate goals.

References

1 Henley Centre for Forecasting 1990 *The Economic Impact of Sport in the UK*. The Sports Council, London (cited in Sport in the Nineties, publication forthcoming).

2 Centre for Leisure Research 1991 *A Digest of Sport Statistics*. The Sports Council, London.

3 Ian Elvin 1986 *The Falcon Club and Sports Complex*. Unpublished report for SASRA.

Further reading

Chris Gratton and Peter Taylor 1985 *Sport and Recreation: An Economic Analysis*. Spon.
Local Government Act 1988 HMSO, London.
George Torkildsen 1992 *Leisure and Recreation Management*. Third Edition, Spon.

9 Facilities for indoor sport and recreation

Introduction

This section seeks to provide a fairly broad overview of facility provision focusing on traditional urban sports activity with a more detailed account to follow. Other texts in this series will enable you to develop your appreciation of facility management. Even though sports and leisure centres have adopted an important place in the supply of cultural services, particularly since they have a relatively recent record. Community provision has a longer history, with many facilities built for multiple usage. Where a resource may have had a defined role, more attention is now being placed on extending the contribution through dual or multi-use. The provision of swimming pools, one of our most traditional sports facilities, remains a high priority for many organisations, including commercial operators like hotel and holiday groups. Outdoor sports in Britain are a part of the established fabric of society, particularly traditional team games; however changes do appear to be taking place. Loss of playing fields, competitive tendering and the continuing role of voluntary sports organisations will all feature in the 1990s.

Although there are many other sports facilities than those mentioned above, the intention is to broaden the reader's understanding regarding facility provision and management. There are also sections in this book which refer to organisations from the public and private sectors. This should certainly broaden understanding of issues that most affect managers in the operation of a good many facilities.

Public and private sectors

Sports facilities for formal and recreational activity are in the control of both public and private sectors. The voluntary sector has long had a special association with the needs of team games, and commercial organisations have long been focusing on specific markets, including health studios and fitness centres. Spectator sports, particularly professional soccer, are another important part of the British sports scene. The complete sports scenario, however, is much more complex than this. Commercial opportunities are continually being pursued. A glance at the winter and summer sports holiday business is a clear indication of growing markets and changing patterns of behaviour. With an increasing number of holiday operators offering activity holidays, trends towards increased participation seem likely to continue. The opportunity for swimming whilst on vacation can determine patterns of behaviour before or after a vacation. Golf, tennis, hill walking, cycling and boating holidays can encourage people into a new activity.

Certain minority sports, like volleyball, are emerging with an increasing pattern of participation. Attitudes towards participation are more flexible than they have been before.

Minority sports have a wonderful opportunity to promote participation through encouraging really positive experiences and creating an attractive image for their sport. Ultimately the nature of any facility, the type of ownership and the market it serves, will largely determine what programmes and services are available to the public. Changes in management emphasis have taken place in recent years, and they seem to have influenced attitudes towards the role of marketing. It is one function of management that professionals agree is critical in a keen competitive environment.

The cost of facility hire and membership constraints will continue to exert an influence over involvement in sport and recreation. There is more to providing access to sport than simply building new facilities. Potential consumers still need the time, the money, the transport and an encouraging social and education background before they make a commitment to participate.

There is no consistency, or agreed standards of facility provision in Britain. Public and private organisations may co-exist just as they can compete for business. Whilst local authorities have tended to consider collective consumption and the satisfaction of need as priorities there are increasing examples of competition for customers. This would seem both understandable and practical where both organisations provide for distinct markets and when the size of that market permits co-existence. Each district or community will therefore demonstrate a distinct character which in itself illustrates local aspirations and market forces.

Facilities and the development of participation

Awareness of participation levels in sport, and of the demand for facilities, has only really emerged over the last 20 years or so. In 1969 two surveys were published, the *Pilot National Recreation Survey*[1] and *Planning for Leisure*.[2] *The General Household Survey* (GHS) began gathering data on sports and recreation activity in 1973 and continued in 1977, 1980, 1983, 1986 and 1990.[3] An examination of such data not only provides an insight into participation, it also provides an opportunity to review trends.

Managers require customer profiles, trends in participation and market forecasting to remain confident of their business strategy. Despite the availability of some data on participation, and the recognition amongst managers that they must understand the markets they serve, we still do not undertake sufficient research on sports participation.

With so much activity taking place in purpose-built facilities, but outside the control of affiliated sports clubs, many governing bodies can only guess at participation rates. Sports such as squash, badminton and tennis are each popular as 'casual' activities and the people who play may not belong to a club or play in recognised competitions.

In 1972 the Sports Council published Provision for Sport,[4] which examined targets for facility development. Those targets based on recommended numbers for sports centres, swimming pools and golf courses have had some effect on development. It was more likely, however, that the prospect of local government reorganisation in 1974 would have a more dramatic effect on facility development. Indeed a number of local authorities took the opportunity to extend facility provision at this time; some without a detailed appreciation of facility design and community needs. The mistakes of the 1970s still haunt us although a number of centres have already required structural adaptation and improvements.

In 1982 the Sports Council redefined facility needs and priorities for the 1980s when considering:

- the refurbishment of old facilities
- more locally-based centres in urban and rural areas
- the improvement of turf pitches[5]

One of the problems associated with recommending targets of facility provision is that they can be seen as meaningless. Without adequate resources, or a legal process, available to back up the estimation of need there is no requirement in law to respond to published priorities.

With financial and political constraints now determining a new role for local authorities, partnerships between sectors are being encouraged. Local authorities can, and do, work with the commercial sector in a variety of often exciting joint ventures.

Opening up education facilities also remains a priority, as indeed it has been for about 30 years since the Wolfenden Committee reported in 1960. Community use of facilities in schools and colleges concerns all those interested in widening access and encouraging participation. Although most managers see themselves serving a community, the recognised gaps in participation and the drop-out rate of children when they leave school remains a problem.

Two methods of promoting better links with education and making better use of facilities are dual use and joint provision. They are not the only means of using or opening up facilities which may be locked up for at least 12 weeks a year but they can make a significant contribution.

Dual use refers to the regular use of facilities by customers other than those for whom they were first intended. Dual use of schools, having previously been administered by local education departments for public use by groups or club members, is now the responsibility of the local management and the headteacher in particular. In the Sports Council study, *Sharing Does Work*,[6] the most important forms of dual use involved cooperation between a local management (the local education authority) and a district recreation authority, or between committees of a metropolitan district. The effect of LMS on participation and dual use has changed since 1990. There is now no controlling influence at the centre and pricing and promotion policies are defined by the schools themselves.

Dual use has both economic and social advantages. Even adaptations to buildings may prove economically sound. Capital costs shared between partners, with revenue expenditure met by the community, can help to persuade the doubters that dual use is beneficial. However, three factors need to be borne in mind.

1 Are the appropriate organisations committed to dual use?
2 Is management aware of local needs and able to respond accordingly?
3 Does the initial investment have a pay back based on economic and social benefits?

Joint provision, involving cooperation between authorities, refers to planning, constructing, even managing, a facility together. In a metropolitan authority this may mean cooperation between committees.

However, Britain continues to lock up too many educational sports facilities during vacation periods. Although some 36 per cent of centres offer a dual use policy, and they provide young people with the opportunity to broaden their sporting interests, there is still much that can be done. For some 30 years the terrible waste of facilities has been recognised and regretted. If there is one area of potential cooperation and collaboration it must surely be in freeing the significant sports facilities in schools, and in institutions of further and higher education. Policy agreements, along with the allocation of responsibility and costs, continue to obstruct progress. The promotion of examples of good practice, made possible by some enlightened authorities, is needed to provoke the political will at a high level. Appropriate investment would offer a significant and worthwhile return.

The physical location of a centre, the quality of access and egress are as fundamental as primary planning criteria. The perception of potential customers towards the social and catering amenity and the diversity of programming must be favourable. Centres are accommodating as many as 30 activities, even though the majority of booking sheets can be dominated by five a side, squash and badminton.

Britain does enjoy the advantage of a fairly well established leisure management profession, well positioned and increasingly experienced to assist the determination of goals for the 1990s. Although a young and emerging profession, leisure managers and leisure organisations are becoming key agents in a dynamic sector of the British economy.

Sports and recreation centres

Over the last 25 years attitudes have changed significantly towards facility objectives, design, the management of opportunity and participation programmes. Prior to the 1960s there were very few indoor sports facilities; local government, now a major provider, had a less influential role. The 1990s, however, sees the public sector owning a very considerable resource including the vast majority of purpose-built facilities.

The growth of indoor provision in Britain, towards a total of approaching 2,500 or so sports and leisure centres, has undoubtedly led to increased participation in sport. Although it is difficult to be precise about the number of indoor sports centres and halls it has been estimated that there are approximately 1,500 in England, 750 in Scotland and in Wales about 120 indoor sports halls.[7,8] The figures for Scotland do not include the many village and community halls. New centres have not, as sometimes feared, put older facilities at risk, and emerging sports like volleyball have enjoyed enhanced growth. Basketball and gymnastics have benefitted from better facilities, while squash and indoor bowls have emerged as leading sports. Squash is catered for in both public and private centres and is seen by managers in both sectors as a potentially profitable activity.

Nevertheless compulsory competitive tendering with the subsequent client and contractor roles, will clearly require a reappraisal of the role of both the public and private sectors, particularly in the response to facility management. Certainly attitudes will change towards design, management and programming. Greater management freedom and flexibility is required in order that facilities and management can reach targets of performance.

With nine million retired people in Britain, and a further three million adults not in work, the concept of a 'leisure society' has moved to centre stage. Those in employment are also likely to have longer holidays, a shorter working week and higher disposable incomes. Prevailing social trends, a growing awareness of positive health and fitness, and greater mobility should increase demand for sport and recreation facilities.

Reorganisation of local government in England and Wales (1974) and in Scotland (1975) resulted in considerable facility development. Recreation departments, or their equivalent, were created to manage expensive 'new' resources. Local authorities pursued an individualistic approach to development influenced by local politics and not always offering clear objectives to centre managers. Programming often reflected local aspirations, sometimes those of the manager, but centres did broaden the range of sports and cultural activities available. Recreationists and managers had started to examine their role critically. There are now many examples of diversified and well oriented multi-purpose centres catering to a wide ranging public. Facilities like the Crowtree Leisure

Centre in Sunderland, Tyne and Wear, offer a wide range of sports activity without neglecting an opportunity to programme other leisure-based events. Nor does the management team neglect the provision of a catering and social amenity as it continues to attract 1.5 million people per year.

Priorities for centre development

The Sports Council, through the Technical Unit for Sport (TUS), makes recommendations regarding size and design of sports centres. Such advice is, however, only used by those who seek it. Thankfully much has improved since the late 1960s and early 1970s when facilities were built without recognising the need to have:

1 Clear objectives.
2 An appreciation of the sportsperson's needs.
3 The needs of management recognised in the design.

The search for meaningful concepts must continue. It is only by thinking about what we are doing that issues emerge and relationships between facilities and the markets they serve become clear.

Too often facilities failed to connect with the needs of the community they were intended to serve.

The voluntary sector relies on the public authorities for facilities while the commercial organisations naturally and understandably design for profit and not for wider community benefit.

Prevailing market forces, professional expertise, political will, economic and social factors have all had a bearing on what is built, where, at what price; and for which particular target group.

Government has given no clear direction in facility development. Local authorities had to establish their own criteria for provision. Central authorities only offered permissive powers and limited grant aid through quasi-independent organisations, or from special project funds.

The 1970s and 1980s witnessed a tendancy for local authorities to offer facilities for sport at subsidised prices, with the commercial sector focusing on the more profitable activities of squash, snooker, health and fitness, bars and catering.

The quality of the facility, access characteristics, and the catchment area for specific activities are clearly central issues in determining markets. Socio-economic factors undoubtedly fashion demand, just as political considerations may influence location, design and programming, particularly in high income areas or in those communities experiencing significant unemployment.

Effective management has become a salient issue; maximising the utilisation of resources and the generation of targeted income are more important now that ever before. The desire for greater community use of local authority facilities, including multi-activity programming, has led to improvements in administration, the introduction of new equipment and technology in monitoring and servicing the needs of the market.

Figure 9.1 Model Diagram illustrating determination of development options

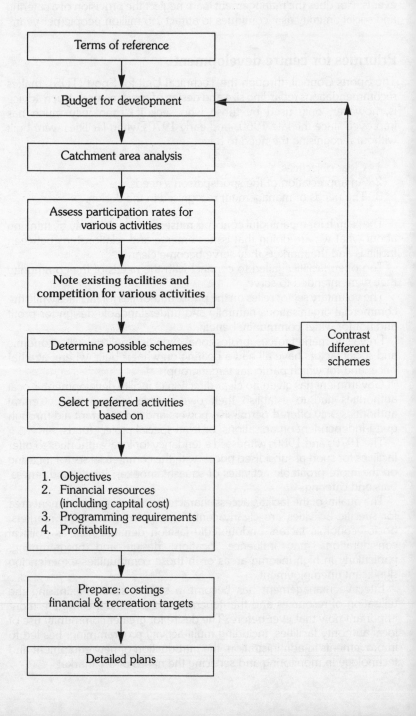

The management of any sports or recreation complex requires specific targets to be set and the determination of a strategic approach if objectives are to be satisfied. Facilities must therefore be designed in order to satisfy the needs of the market they serve. A strategic plan must identify the facility requirements, namely: What ? Where ? When ? How ?

The model diagram, Figure 9.1, follows a process of enquiry where managers need to specifically address their information requirements. At strategic moments there is a need to compare or contrast different schemes based on the original terms of reference. Although an element of judgement or appraisal will always be required there is a fundamental need to make decisions based on the right information.

The model defines a progression which is determined by the successful outcome of the previous stage. Although alternative models exist the same critical dimensions appear on most of them. Planning facility development is a matter for professional skill and judgement. Discussion surrounding the need for a sports facility will have to respond to declared objectives and a budget that recognises revenue costs and capital costs. All facilities must achieve one goal, they must satisfy needs and provide a service that recognises the importance of quality and customer care.

Partnerships

When considering the feasibility of a project, financial constraints are always a limiting factor. Partners who might share either the cost of a facility, or the purpose for which it was built, should be regarded carefully. There are now a number of developments in Britain where local authority collaboration with a retail organisation has enabled a capital project to go ahead. The Rainbow Centre near Middlesbrough is a well designed example of this. Development costs provided from the commercial company coupled with access to local authority owned land, and with planning permission, makes the prospect of a joint project more than just a pipe dream. The anticipation of planning gain, from a development in their area, which is greater than the commercial project alone, is something local authorities need to consider seriously. There are associated problems, however, particularly if planning permission becomes dependent on unfavourable conditions being met.

The possibility of adapting old buildings, once so much in vogue, should always be examined. With ideal sites at a premium a project team might well contemplate joining a wider development. Capital costs for a conversion can be prohibitive but prime sites in large conurbations are difficult to find.

Phasing a project over a period of time to enable future extensions, or creating a flexible facility capable of multi-activity, are further ways in which managers and planners can be proactive in their responses to future needs.

It is difficult to accurately define the quality of sport facility provision in Great Britain. There is such a diversity of type and location that various national, regional or area statistics are being used to quantify standards. Not only are there no agreed bench marks to measure by, there are varying degrees of influence between a number of factors including:

1   Public and private sectors.
2   Size and character of local authority.
3   Strength of local voluntary organisations.
4   Economic strength of the area, incorporating commercial prospects.
5   Socio-cultural characteristics which may be influenced by the geographical area or region.
6   Regional and national trends in facility provision.

The development of facilities for sport and recreation has gone through a period of fairly rapid growth. Although the rate of expansion did slow down during the mid 1980s current trends in development are marked by an increasing number of partnerships between public and private sectors, and by the influence and effect of compulsory competitive tendering.

Facility development and facility management will be required to pursue a more meaningful and objective assessment of effectiveness in the future. This could in turn lead to an increasing emphasis on leisure and fun activities with sport and recreation assuming a lesser role.

Standardised Approach to Sports Halls (SASH)

Many changes have taken place over the last 20 years, particularly in the design and operation of public authority sports facilities. Managers have had to come to terms with diverse needs, new sports and their technical requirements, and the constantly changing political climate. Although special schemes need not be a panacea, there are occasions when particular projects can teach everyone a lesson or two. Although not without its critics, the Standardised Approach to Sports Halls (SASH) offered a positive contribution to the development of facility design. The SASH centres have been geared to serving catchment populations of about 25,000 people. Inspired by a partnership between the Sports Council and Bovis, the project managers, the Standardised Approach to Sports Halls seeks to service a defined community with as many as seventeen sports, including:

Badminton	Indoor hockey	Roller disco
Basketball	Judo	Roller skating
Bowls	Karate	Table tennis
Cricket nets	Keep fit	Trampolining
Five-a-side soccer	Movement and dance	Volleyball
Olympic gymnastics	Netball	

Being able to programme a wide variety of sports activity, and maintaining a keen control on costs, have become important features of a manager's profile. SASH schemes cater for 100,000 user visits per annum and are geared to keep operating costs to a minimum.[9]

In addition to the hall, equivalent to four badminton courts, SASH can also provide spectator facilities, a fitness training room, a reception and social area, and changing accommodation. Limited choice on finish keeps building costs to a minimum. Squash and swimming facilities come as optional extras.

Different local authorities have adopted alternative approaches based on identified local need. Variations in design have been used to emphasise the social programme, including entertainments and special events.

The development of community-based provision has largely replaced the building of major sports and recreation complexes. Costs became prohibitive and local authorities found themselves working in a very different political climate to that of the 1970s and early 1980s. Just as SASH provided an operational model of a smaller low cost facility, the encouragement through the late 1980s and early 1990s has been on flexible, multi use, locally-based, low-cost, easy to manage facilities.

Where local authorities previously offered little indoor sports facility, it has been possible for some networking of community centres to take place. The City of Durham, for example, has pursued an outreach policy locating a number of facilities in outlying communities. Although the officers and members prepared their own, in house, design specifications similar management principles were used to those in the SASH project.

This chapter has largely focused on design, facility development and management, and SASH provides an insight into one type of facility provision. Current trends towards positive health and fitness, and the continuing impact of wet facilities as a major resource leads us to consider health based facilities and swimming pools.

Health-based facilities

Public awareness of positive health, personal image and life style has in recent years improved perceptions towards health based facilities. In 1979 the Sports Council published a study on leisure pools[10] in which they concluded that the use made of the solarium and the sauna was modest.

Trends in leisure can change dramatically and since the early 1980s health-based products and activities have enjoyed increased demand.

There have been significant improvements and extensions to the products and services available. A greater number of companies now operate in the leisure business and managers need to consider carefully how, if at all, they should provide these facilities.

Customers may seek a package of activity, including sports participation with utilisation of health facilities. The availability of a sauna, sunbed or spa may directly influence a decision to play squash, work out in the fitness room, or swim in a particular centre. From a marketing point of view there are clear advantages to be made from persuading potential customers to spend more of their time and money at one centre.

The manager must consider a number of factors when offering advice concerning the development of a health resource namely:

1 What amenities are required, and what will they cost?
2 How will the public access the facilities and how will this affect centre programming?
3 What are the maintenance and supervision requirements?
4 What kind of environment is necessary to house the amenities?
5 What kind of financial return can be expected in terms of income per square metre, income per customer and income per facility?

Whatever the buying decision, from £4,000 for a sauna, £11,000 for a spa system, or £5,000 for a high pressure UVA sunbed, safety will always be a top priority.

Health-based equipment is increasingly being associated with aerobic and anaerobic programmes of activity. Dance studios, with adjacent weights and 'work out' facilities, can, with a health suite, provide an integrated package catering to the needs of specific target markets. Carefully designed and well managed, they can also provide attractive returns on investment capital.

Swimming pools

Swimming pools have for many years been seen as the ideal facility to get fit and keep healthy. Developments in facility provision during the mid-nineteenth century were based in the belief that the working class needed facilities for personal hygiene and that the public should be offered the discipline of swimming as a purposeful activity.

Since the mid 1970s pools have been subject to technological developments, and consumers are often able to choose between a traditional pool environment or a free form leisure pool. Facility development has remained primarily in the public sector, but commercial operations have been encouraged to provide swimming facilities. Superior hotels, and the tourist business in particular, have made a contribution to facility development even if facilities are not always open to the general public.

Over recent years certain life styles and attitudes have changed. The home environment has become a primary leisure resource, and it has become necessary for the leisure management profession to promote attractive, stimulating and comfortable environments if the potential customer is to be persuaded away from domestic bliss. Swimming pools have become sporting, recreational and leisure environments. Indeed, a visit to a modern leisure pool may confirm that few customers will actually be swimming. Playing on the beach, jumping into the waves, spiralling down the aquaslide or relaxing at the poolside cafe can provide alternative attractions.

In 1972 the Sports Council published *Provision for Sport* in which the criteria of 2.72 square metres of water area per bather was used as a means to judge future facility requirements.[11] The recommendation was for 450 new pools to be provided in England before 1981. Local government re-organisation, coupled with a more progressive attitude towards provision, led to this national target being achieved. Between 1973 and 1977 swimming pool provision increased by 70 per cent with 190 new pools being built in 1973-74 alone.

Sports Council targets were redrawn with the publication of *Sport in the Community, The Next Ten Years*, where it was recognised that adequate information was required if accurate forecasting was to be published.[12] It was foreseen that 200 older pools should be refurbished and 50 new pools built all before 1988.

In the more recent strategy document *Sport in the Community, Into the 90s*,[13] the Sports Council again recognises the inadequacy of available information on patterns of pool provision. A detailed report was published in 1983 which sought to overcome this difficulty – namely *Swimming in the Community*, (National Swimming Pools Study, The Sports Council, London).[14] The outcome of this work was to persuade the Sports Council that local authorities did not share their aspirations towards undertaking swimming pool refurbishments. Replacement pools were a more likely prospect, with leisure pools gaining popular support. Financial constraints were increasing but the political will, and the influence of the consumer, were clearly important. With the 50 new pools target already achieved in 1984 and 144 new facilities since 1982, targets were clearly unrealistic.

With a modest hotel pool costing at least 150,000, investment decisions need to be weighed up very carefully. The emphasis given in any judgement will depend on the character of the organisation. Economic, social and political decisions will be made based on the established terms of reference. Construction costs for a 25 metre pool, with a 250 square metre area, are approximately 1 million. Consideration of wider facility development, and recurring revenue expenditure, necessitates careful deliberation at the feasibility stage.

Achieving target income figures is bound up in satisfying customers. We have already seen a change from swimming to recreational activities; the transition may now be towards 'fun'. In exploring future demands and in recognising significant technological improvements, managers are increasingly likely to consider the place of wave machines, aquaslides, geysers, waterfalls and compressed air systems.

Compulsory competitive tendering may change the emphasis even further. Certainly one major concern of the Amateur Swimming Association is the effect CCT may have on the provision of facilities for swimming. ASA anxiety has been expressed about the effects of leisure pools on the nation's ability to swim.[15] A continued push towards achieving economic targets can only exacerbate those who fear a shift in management philosophy and an extension towards more leisure pools at the expense of traditional pools.

A National Strategy for Swimming and Swimming Pool Provision, published in 1992, estimated that there were about 1,300 public indoor pools in the UK in 1991.[16] It has also been determined that nearly 2,500 primary and over 850 secondary schools have their own pool.[17] As with other sports facilities it is important that quality is maintained and that facilities are refurbished to maintain acceptable standards. It is estimated in the national strategy that the current supply of swimming pools will require approximately 1,200 million of re-investment during the 1990s. Constraints on local authority finances may result in many pools being closed rather than being modernised. Swimming pools capable of holding competitions require 25 metre or 50 metre facilities. In 1991 there were 11 pools suited to long course championships, with only three being opened since 1970. The Ponds Forge International Centre in Sheffield now stands out as the finest competition swimming facility in The UK. The national strategy notes that Scotland and Northern Ireland require a 50 metre facility and that diving, water polo and synchronised swimming have poor facilities in which to train and compete. Apart from the quantity and accuracy of available data, two issues seem pertinent.

1 Local government in Britain is not guided by Sports Council or ASA targets.
2 Central government does not provide sufficient resources to enable a national programme to take place.

In France the 'Mille Piscine', and in Germany the 'Golden Plan', were each geared towards a national development of swimming facilities. Comparisons between different systems of government are impractical here, but these examples do provide an indication of national intent. Decisions taken at a policy level with investment capital in prospect are much more encouraging.

One of the more interesting problems faced by local authorities, all over the country, concerns the continued operation of the older pools. Many of these older pools still exist, in fact 140 pools identified in the 1982 Sports Council strategy for closure remain open. It is likely that about 11 pools have been refurbished, but many remain expensive to operate with little prospect of renovation. The most likely outcomes are closure, or closure with a replacement pool. Over recent years one in four new facilities have been leisure pools, with the overall figure closer to one in ten. ASA concern appears to be justified, as is the widespread anxiety surrounding the future management of local authority swimming pool provision.

Standards of provision have never been set in Britain for any sports facility. Suggested targets can be little more than a guide to the adequacy or shortfall of provision. Certainly the Sports Council's advice has been necessary and useful, but one questions what positive outcome has emerged from recognising that there should be one 25 metre pool and one learner pool for every 40,00 to 45,000 people.

Such a conclusion is reaffirmed through the Regional Councils for Sport and Recreation who, when asked to contribute a local view to the National Swimming Pools Study, concluded that each area was different.[18] Access arrangements and the nature of pool requirements must also be determined by regional circumstances particularly when looking at pool sizes. The different sizes that can be considered are: neighbourhood pool; district pool; sub regional pool; regional pool; and national facility. Swimming needs must be determined according to demand for recreational swimming; teaching of swimming; organised swimming; training and competitive swimming.

The possibility that new pools will continue to be added and old pools will be refurbished must be seen in relation to 1993 and beyond when, with continued constraint on local authority budgets, and the prospect of having to go to competitive tender for facility management many authorities may elect to focus their sport programmes elsewhere. This could seriously effect the prospects for facility development. Education facilities have been excluded from CCT, although spending constraints remain, and there is no guarantee that grant maintained status will enable the opt out schools to be grant aided by central government to build a swimming pool.

Leisure pools

The emphasis on recreation and leisure in pool design dates back to 1974 when the Bletchley, Herringthorpe (Rotherham) and Whitley Bay pools were opened. Free form pools, based on a variation of the 25 metre facility, can be used to suit both the needs of the serious swimmer and those who swim for fun. The early influence on design came from the Summerland project in Tokyo, with its wave-making machine, landscaping, beaches and the facility to hold a range of poolside events. German successes in the 1980s brought us flume rides, and multiple slides.

The challenge to leisure architects in the 1990s is to continue, wherever possible, to harmonise the needs of the serious swimmer with the wider needs of a leisure market. Competitive swimming is, however, governed by rules which offer considerable constraints when designing a free form pool. During the 1970s and 1980s the needs of serious swimmers tended to be met by separate pools: learners in the small teaching pool and the more experienced in the main pool. Facilities also moved to metric sizes, 25 metres, 33.3 metres or 50 metres, with spectator seating appropriate to local needs. Leisure pools tended to encourage not just swimming but a diversity of activity.

Although pools offer a tremendously versatile and positive contribution to leisure activity generally, and sport and recreation in particular, they remain very expensive facilities. Energy costs can be as much as one third of the running costs. It also takes four times as much energy to operate a swimming pool as a building of similar design. Managers must be concerned to save energy costs wherever possible, especially through use of pool covers, efficient boilers, improved air ventilation and heat recovery systems.

Significant savings can be made, even in excess of 70 per cent. The long-term benefits of new technology are, subject to investment appraisal, a likely area for saving.

The challenge for swimming pool managers through the 1990s must be to maintain high standards of customer care, recognise diverse needs and always offer a safe, clean and exciting environment in which to swim, either seriously or recreationally, or to just have fun.

Summary of key points

1 Participation in sport and recreation has increased over the last ten years for a number of reasons. More facilities available for wet and dry activities is certainly one important factor. Other reasons include a more positive attitude to health and fitness, greater provision of coaching courses which seek to encourage participation and a willingness on the part of the provider to make the experience both attractive and enjoyable.

2 This section has sought to illustrate the trends in facility provision over recent years and to highlight some of the issues that will concern managers during the 1990s. The public sector having completed the competitive tendering process in 1993 became less inclined to finance new sports complexes. Great Britain is, however, providing a model for facility development in Europe by encouraging partnerships between public and private sectors. With advantages to both the tax payer and the sports-minded such partnerships are set to continue. Facility development has become so expensive that links with developers, who also seek to ensure the development of community based facilities, has distinct financial attractions. A local authority might receive a sports centre for little or no capital payment and the developer manages to build commercial or retail facilities. It might have cost the local authority some land, but they have control through the planning responsibility and can determine the benefits, for example, of a retail and recreational development.

3 With greater choice and, in many areas, the money to enjoy leisure activities the customer can expect to benefit from improved quality control, better customer care and keen competition.

4 Swimming pools have made an important contribution to the development of sport and recreation, particularly since the 1970s when the concept of leisure pools was accepted. Facilities for swimming, and recreational bathing, have continued to play a pre-eminent role in the determination of trends and patterns of participation. Technology has played a part, but so has the desire for a fun experience. In some water based facilities, particularly the more recent buildings with sophisticated and innovative equipment, it is possible to go to a pool but not actually do any swimming. With all the action being confined to the slides, rides, geysers and waves there may be little or no desire for the traditional activity. Wet facilities set the standards in facility provision earlier in the century and they seem to be setting the style for the 1990s.

5 Changing perceptions regarding the desire for quality of recreational

experience are likely to continue. Experiences gained on vacation at commercially run facilities are increasingly likely to be mirrored in the more traditional urban settings.

6 Renovations and refurbishments of facilities might not be the cheap alternative some imagine, particularly if the character of provision is expected to fit a particular image.

   If the Tropicana water based leisure facility in Rotterdam is at all typical in attracting 600,000 people a year paying at least £4 for admission the pattern seems to be firming towards commercially oriented entertaining facilities.

7 Compulsory competitive tendering, changes in attitudes and an increase in participation will be dynamic forces in the 1990s. It remains to be seen if the quality of sport, and the development of excellence, can keep pace with change. There are governing bodies who see grey clouds ahead with the decline in standards and an increase in costs high in their list of concerns.

In order to bring some of the fundamental management issues into focus a case study of one leisure centre in Carlisle, Cumbria will highlight the development of one concept into a reality.

Case Study: The Sands Centre, Carlisle, Cumbria.

The Sands Centre, opened in 1985, is an excellent local authority facility in the North West of England which provides us with an example of project development (see Figure 9.2). It is not intended that the previous diagram should be mirrored here. Local circumstances are always likely to cause slight variations.

The original policy of those planning the centre was that it should cover all aspects of leisure and recreation, including sport, art and entertainment.

A multi-functional centre – the architect's brief
It was the architect's aim to provide flexibility within the physical structure of the centre, in order to allow all forms of events to take place. An example of this was retractable seating. It was also intended that many facilities should have a secondary as well as a primary function. For example, a squash court could be adapted into an extra changing room, or an additional exhibition room.

In 1980, when planning first began in the form of the 'Sparts' project, it was estimated that the centre would cost in the region of 6.6 million. The final figure was more in the region of 16 million for the Sands Centre.

The final product consisted of a 1.5 court sports hall capable of seating 1,500 people. The second smaller hall can be used as a separate facility or as an overspill facility for events held in the main hall. There are also bars and small entertainment areas.

The centre is sited to the north of Carlisle next to the river Eden. This also made it close to other facilities for golf and athletics. The river, however, imposed certain structural limitations on the centre. The Sands Centre has good access and egress as well as adequate parking facilities. The design was based on work done using the Acropolis computer in Manchester and this quickened much of the architect's work. For example, it helped in the structuring of seating contours to ensure optimal

Figure 9.2   Model of centre development - planning

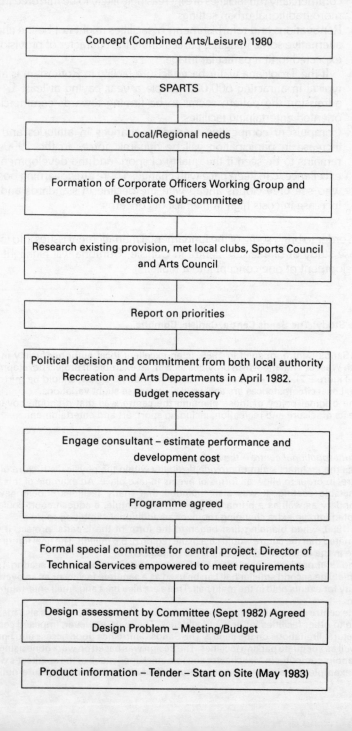

Concept (Combined Arts/Leisure) 1980

SPARTS

Local/Regional needs

Formation of Corporate Officers Working Group and Recreation Sub-committee

Research existing provision, met local clubs, Sports Council and Arts Council

Report on priorities

Political decision and commitment from both local authority Recreation and Arts Departments in April 1982. Budget necessary

Engage consultant – estimate performance and development cost

Programme agreed

Formal special committee for central project. Director of Technical Services empowered to meet requirements

Design assessment by Committee (Sept 1982) Agreed Design Problem – Meeting/Budget

Product information – Tender – Start on Site (May 1983)

views for visitors from all parts of the hall. The computer provided visual designs as well as numerical assessments. The centre was designed so that people with a disability did not have any problems using the facilities, as only facilities which were secondary to activities were placed on the first floor.

The centre was built during a 78 week period (the time of the contract) from May 1983. The manager was appointed one year ahead to assist architecture and design, and this led to the incorporation of a health centre within the complex. The architect expressed disappointment that the overlap was not longer and that he would have preferred to have more contact with the centre staff after it was opened. The Sands Centre was opened in March 1985.

Philosophy of use
The objectives of the council were 'To provide as wide a range of facilities as possible within the budget set in order to answer local and regional community needs'.[19]

The centre received full backing from the Treasury in the Audit Commissioner's Report and this illustrated the good cooperation with the council.

The Sands Centre aimed to provide facilities for three groups of people (See Figure 9.3). These were people requiring:

Figure 9.3 Sands Centre: programming

Monday		Sport
Tuesday	}	and
Wednesday		Recreation
Friday	}	
Saturday		Arts Promotions
Thursday	}	
Sunday		Flexible

1 Recreation and sporting facilities
   As well as providing facilities within all the 'normal' demand areas, e.g. badminton, squash, five-a-side, etc., particular attention was paid to the family groups who would be using the centre e.g. creches. Fewer 'sporting' and more 'recreational' facilities were also provided, e.g. roller-disco and sauna.

2 *Conference and exhibitions*
   The needs of people requiring conferences or exhibition facilities were taken into account in the design of the centre. Examples include greater seating flexibility for conferences and access for large vehicles into the main hall for large items in exhibitions.

3 *Entertainment*
   The promotion of the Arts at the Sands Centre was regarded as a main aim right from the early planning stage. This was because there was no existing provision for the Arts in Carlisle. Good acoustics and excellent access and egress to and from the inside of the centre, together with excellent lighting facilities were provided for the Arts.

With regard to the existing facilities in Carlisle, the Sands Centre attempted to take over many of the bookings previously held by the old Market Hall, as this was no longer considered for recreation and leisure. The centre did not seek to compete with the existing Sports Centre in Carlisle.

Indeed it was decided that the two centres should cooperate and not duplicate the type of facility or activity. This illustrates council cooperation again.

It was intended that the main hall be used 60 per cent of the time for sport and recreation and that the remaining time went towards other promotions. Such promotions were often held at the weekends (for example, concerts and exhibitions). The second hall was intended to be used 90 per cent of the time for sport and recreation. Neither figure was adhered to rigidly, they merely remained as guides. There was restricted club use and more casual session use, where the attitude was an informal 'turn up and join in'.

Sports centre development, a briefing guide
Managers, as well as architects, need to be aware of the elements which make up a brief (See Figure 9.4). Before considering any detail the project team must:

1 Examine time and cost constraints.
2 Consider the operational management characteristics of the centre.
3 Be appraised of specific design factors, including environmental considerations.

Figure 9.4 Summary of briefing guide

Objections of project	Policy
Nature of demand	
Resource availability	
Constraints	
Activity programme	Operational
Staff structure	management
Servicing staff agencies	characteristics
Communications	
Character of enviroment	Design
Specific facility needs	factors
Site conditions	
Fixtures and fittings	
Transport/access infrastructure	
Cost implications	

The Sands Centre remains a successful facility, one which has gained national recognition for the quality of its management. There are distinct advantages for facility managers who have a clear view of their objectives, the role of their facility and the needs of their customers.

References

1 H B Rodgers 1969 *British Pilot National Recreation Survey*. British Travel Association, University of Keele.
2 K K Sillitoe 1969 *Planning for Leisure*. Government Social Survey, HMSO, London.

3 Office of Population Censuses and Surveys 1990 *General Household Survey*. HMSO, London.
4 The Sports Council 1972 *Provision for Sport*.
5 The Sports Council 1982 *Sport in the Community: The Next Ten years*.
6 Cooper and Lybrand 1981 *Sharing does work*. Study 21, The Sports Council, London.
7 Scottish Sports Council 1989 *Sport 2000*. Scottish Sports Council, Edinburgh.
8 Sports Council for Wales 1991 *Changing Times – Changing Needs*. Sports Council for Wales, Cardiff.
9 ECOTECH Research and Consultancy Ltd 1988 *SASH Centres in use*. The Sports Council, London.
10 Public Attitude Surveys Ltd 1979 *Leisure Pools Study 19*. The Sports Council, London.
11 The Sports Council 1972 *Provision for Sport*.
12 The Sports Council 1982 *Sport in the Community, The Next Ten Years*.
13 The Sports Council 1988 *Sport in the Community, Into the 90s*.
14 The Sports Council 1983 *Swimming in the Community*.
15 Amateur Swimming Association ASA 1988 *Annual Report*.
16 Kit Campbell Associations 1992 *Provision for Swimming: A National Strategy for Swimming and Swimming Provision*. The Sports Council, London.
17 Department of Education and Science 1992 *Results of a Survey of school based swimming pools. Unpublished report cited in Sport in the Nineties – New Horizons*.
18 The Sports Council 1983 *Swimming in the Community*.
19 Carlisle DC, 1985 ILAM Seminar (Unpublished notes).

Further reading

G John 1981 *A Handbook of Sports Design*. Architectural Press.
The Sports Council Annual Reports.

10 Facilities for outdoor sport and recreation

Introduction

Britain has long been regarded as a nation enthusiastic about outdoor team sports. National sports, like soccer, rugby, and cricket are all major outdoor team games. The inference from this might be that we are well supplied with outdoor playing facilities. A number of constraints, however, have been recognised, notably the lack of publicly available outdoor sports facilities. The NPFA and the CCPR have each been taking a keen interest in this issue, seeking to maintain or establish links with organisations who may be experiencing difficulty either in securing pitches to play on or by being threatened with the sale of the grounds they seek to use.

Upward trends in participation, in selected sports, have exacerbated the problem. The Sports Council strategy, published in 1988,[1] acknowledged the difficulty of quantifying the precise character of provision for outdoor sports facilities. This comes after the previous strategy document, published in 1982, which identified a need for 3,000 new or refurbished playing pitches, 600 of which were required in areas of special need.[2] It is generally estimated that there are approximately 70,000 pitches in England, about 4,000 in Scotland with, as yet, no clear indication or estimate of the number in Wales. As pressure on urban open space continues, and as more and more playing fields are sold for development, there is every reason for anxiety. The CCPR and the NPFA have openly voiced their concern for what is irrecoverable loss of land. Yet as demand for sport is being generally encouraged no quantification of need is available except at a local level. Here standards are inconsistently applied. Increased concern regarding the levels of playing field provision has resulted in a government grant of 500,000 to establish a Register of Recreational Land in England. There is also a real need for locally based assessment of demand to be applied consistently across the country; for example the North West Council for Sport and Recreation considered their strategy requirements through a cast study based in St. Helens.[3]

The advice contained in the report that followed urges the adoption of a methodological approach which needs to be applied locally. Local standards were more insightful than a nationally derived figure. Such studies will need to consider using pitches as a unit of supply rather than total hectares/acres inclusive of ancillary space. Maximum and minimum sizes of pitches as defined by the governing body clearly imply the possibility of a variation in total number.

The National Playing Fields Association in specifying a standard of six acres of outdoor playing space per 1000 population do include children's formal and informal play areas.[4] The figure for youth and adult use in the public, private, commercial and industrial sectors is four to 4.5 acres. Exclusions from the NPFA recommendations are school playing fields (unless specifically designed for full joint use), 9 and eighteen hole golf courses, grounds of Her Majesty's Services, large areas of water and verges, woodland commons and parks (not defined as playing space).

Returning to the report from the North West Regional Council, it was the conclusion of the planning team that the NPFA model was a useful guide which required local application. It is worth noting that the NWCSR report published in 1982 was followed by the NPFA six acre target review in 1986. One problem experienced by all those involved in determining local standards is the role of school playing fields. If facilities are used by clubs they should be included. This seems an eminently sensible approach to the matter.

A case study based on the possible loss of playing fields appeared in Chapter 7. Although attitudes to the need for adequate playing space do appear to be developing, it may only be as a result of losing many urban sports grounds that a locally-based standards approach will be generally recognised. The publication and influence of the Department of Environment's planning policy guide-line (PPG17), which places a value on sports provision and encourages a keen eye on protecting facilities in an urban environment, should go some way to highlighting need when planning applications are considered.

The availability of adequate space is a limiting factor in the consideration of outdoor sports facilities. It is also important to recognise that access, location and distribution are significant variables. It may already be too late, however, for many of our larger towns and cities to achieve a minimum standard. Certainly it is relatively unlikely that limited open space, not currently used for sport, would be retained to accommodate potential future demand. The majority of sports and recreational activities take place in a preferred social setting. Reduce the quality of the physical and social environment and people may not continue to participate.

The trend of the 1980s could well continue through the 1990s, namely a continuing loss of playing field space in urban environments. There is likely to be encouragement to replace urban sports fields with available land on the fringes of our towns and cities. Although similar facilities can be provided and profits from land development offer additional security, there could be problems. Sportsmen and women previously used to a local facility may opt out of travelling five to eight miles to their 'new' club. Younger girls and boys may find the prospect of starting to play sports with a club out of town distinctly less attractive. Parents may be less inclined to support such participation. The cost of travel, both in time and money, will also act as a discouragement to those who possibly lack the resources.

Although the development of urban fringe areas will occur, and this may be of benefit to large numbers of people, it cannot totally replace the community-based urban facilities. Local authorities can seek to achieve locally determined standards by encouraging the development and use of multi purpose areas, but careful consideration should be given to any trend which might have a negative effect on participation. Rural areas with small population figures have a different problem. If a community lacks the population to support a facility, individuals may have to travel to the urban sports clubs. Alternatively, rural populations of less than 1000 may have a sports field which implies a level of provision greater than that used in the cities, or encouraged by the NPFA. The development of opportunities in rural areas requires cooperation between organisations like the Sports Council and the Countryside Commission, particularly in areas of mutual interest such as the development of Country Parks and water resources for sport and recreation.

Current issues include the amount of investment required to maintain the nation's footpaths and bridleways and the consequences of privatising water which could effect all who have an interest in the countryside. Sensitive planning will be required if attempts at cooperation are to be meaningful.

Artificial surfaces

A number of factors have contributed to the development of synthetic surfaces for outdoor sports activities:

- reduction of available recreation land
- increased demand for outdoor sports facilities
- greater intensity of use afforded by synthetic surfaces
- high standards of performance
- safe playing conditions
- satisfactory maintenance costs
- suitability for all weather conditions

Artificial surfaces have been used for some time. In particular tarmacadam and asphalt have been providing sports facilities for years. The emphasis in recent years has been on more effective use of resources, and there is no doubt that greater intensity of use achieves that. Value for money has become a critical factor in the examination of a recreational asset.

However, artificial turf, as it is commonly known, has been used since the 1960s. In its early days considerable comment was aroused about the quality of performance. Early products have been superseded; even those introduced in the early 1980s are now seen as somewhat inferior when compared to recent developments in the industry.

Figure 10.1   Provision of artificial grass pitches (In excess of 5,000 sq. m.), 1988

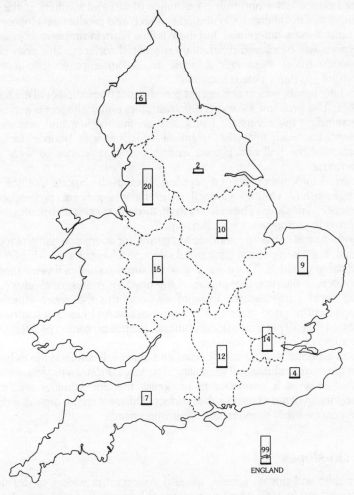

Source: The Sports Council, 1985. Artificial Grass Surfaces-for Soccer, Hockey and Multi-Games Areas – State of the Art. The Sports Council (unpublished), Regional Facilities Data.

There are advantages for some sports, like cricket, which virtually guarantee the worthiness of artificial turf. From an organisational point of view more sport can be provided at lower cost. Whilst the character of the playing surfaces is clearly different from grass, the prospect of a guaranteed ready-made cricket wicket enhances the opportunity to increase participation and improve standards. Grass pitches will continue to have a prime role in the provision of outdoor sports facility, but we have yet to see the fulfilment of the potential for artificial turf.

The bounce factor and rolling resistance of turf and synthetic surfaces remain distinctly different. Continued research and product development may reduce these differences, but there is little harm in simply recognising that sports will be played differently on artificial surfaces. This does not necessarily make them less valuable as activities, particularly if the opportunity to participate is increased.

Hockey, tennis, soccer and cricket can all profit from additional artificial facilities. The problem for sports administrators and managers is actually understanding the diversity of products on the market, and acquiring sufficient knowledge of the technical specifications; bounce factor, resilience of the ball and player, friction burns, resistance to wear or temperature.

Detailed information can be supplied through the Sports Council or Nottinghamshire County Council, who have significant professional experience in this area. The industry itself, through specific companies, will also provide performance specifications.

Synthetic turf can accommodate ten games for every one game played on grass, but it is important that careful selection takes place from the 60 or so available products. There are at least 20 suppliers with a diverse range of products, a situation that promotes the need for professional advice.

The Sport Turf Research Institute also confirms that more effective management of good grass and soil was necessary. Indeed, it has been suggested that 40 per cent of local authority pitches presented problems of inadequate or inefficient drainage.

Local authorities, governing bodies and clubs will continue the debate about the comparability and suitability of surfaces. From an organisational point of view, it is important to recognise the opportunities and the constraints involved in using either surface. Different sports organisations will almost certainly demonstrate contrasting needs.

Dry ski-slopes

The public and private sectors are also important providers of dry ski-slopes; indeed in 1991 there were some 99 dry ski-slopes in operation. Recent financial difficulties experienced by some private ski-slopes suggest the market needs to be reassessed and consideration given to the overall quality of the amenity. The upgrading and extension of facilities may be necessary for survival.

Athletics tracks

Local authorities continue to be the main supplier of athletics tracks; in 1992 there were over 400 athletic tracks in England, 49 in Scotland and 24 in Wales.[5,6] One imminent problem is likely to be the need for a resurfacing programme which is required every 7-10 years. Some concern must be expressed regarding the availability of money in local authorities to undertake adequate maintenance and refurbishment.

Golf courses

The UK has approximately 2000 golf courses, with an average of one facility for every 31,000 people. The recommended figure of one facility for every 25,000 is certainly matched in Scotland where there is one facility for every 12,000 people, but generally there is a shortfall of some 700 new 18 hole golf courses. Many clubs have waiting lists of at least five years and with such lists even being closed as full it is apparent that there is a real need; particularly for pay-as-you-play golf. A number of exclusive golf facilities have recently suffered from their own high costs and the economic downturn.

Stadia

Just as the UK has proportionately less artificial turf facilities than some of our European neighbours, so there is also a relative lack of stadia and stadia managers. Much of the provision in fact lies in professional sports, particularly soccer. Gate-taking sports clubs offer the great majority of stadia in the UK. Modern stadia do have to assume a multi purpose role, particularly if they are to be cost effective. Gateshead International Stadium, widely known for hosting athletics meetings and championships, has also hosted rock concerts, representative rugby and soccer.

The *Handbook of Sports and Recreational Buildings* defines a stadium thus:

> A stadium is a pitch or track for athletics or team competition in an area surrounded by rising stepped tiers for the accommodation of standing or seated spectators, with coverings that do not however, cover the field to enclose the whole building.[7]

An increasing tendency amongst the more forward thinking professional football clubs has been to diversify not just into other major events but also into community based schemes. Flexible, well used community based facilities will become a fact of life for many more stadia managers over the next few years.

Some organisations have sought to broaden the range of products or services available by incorporating an artificial turf facility.

Governing bodies will also continue to exert an influence over the character and design of sports facilities. Some sports, like athletics, may need changing accommodation for over 500 competitors, whereas association football only requires changing facilities for 35 to 40 players.

Managers, when considering the character of a stadium, need to bear the following points in mind:

- good visibility from all parts of the ground
- adequate safety for spectators and players
- good access arrangements, including transportation
- comfortable and attractive accommodation
- flexible design suited to hosting a variety of events
- economic regarding capital expenditure and 'recurring' maintenance costs

Spectator events will need to offer a quality environment with the emphasis on customer care. It will no longer be good enough to provide a quality playing surface and minimal spectator comfort.

Figure 10.2   Pitch Provision in the Northern Region Assisted Financially by the Sports Council and the Football Trust, 1983-1987

■ New pitches
31 soccer
2 hockey
1 rugby, and 2 training areas
9 cricket

■ Artificial surfaces/all purpose areas
32 non-turf cricket wickets
31 multi-purpose games areas
1 artificial grass pitch

■ Other improvements
20 major drainage schemes
8 floodlighting schemes

Source: The Sports Council. (unpublished), Regional Facilities Data.

Summary of key points

1 Not only are private (commercial, voluntary and industrial) organisations selling off playing fields for development, so too are local education authorities. Central government has made it necessary for local authorities to identify land surplus to requirements. As a consequence of falling school rolls during the late 1980s and early 1990s, and in association with accompanying school closures, recreational land has been identified as surplus and has been sold by LEAs. The major problem facing those concerned with the promotion of sport and recreation is that there is no clear accurate evidence of changes, proposed or actual, to the UK supply of outdoor playing fields. Perhaps there is some comfort in the fact that artificial grass pitches in the country have increased from about

30 in 1982 to over 280 today; which is also an increase of over 180 since 1988

Whereas some are owned privately, the majority are in public ownership. The need for research data in this is a matter of some urgency and one hopes that the national register being prepared by the Sports Council will be used to best effect. Data gathered at a local and regional level with consistency in the methodological approach promises to be highly relevant. Associated research also needs to look at demographic trends over a longer period than the next five years. Obstacles to wider use of educational facilities must also be pursued and removed. Improvements to badly drained fields must be made and additional artificial turf facilities should be built in areas of greatest need.

If there is a limit to what can be done regarding new resources then every effort should be made to ensure that public and private organisations make the most of what they have already. In the local authority sector, and as a consequence of PPG17, recreational land can be retained for sport by an internal transfer from an LEA to the appropriate leisure services department.

2 The encouragement towards cooperation, collaboration and partnerships between organisations continues as the emphasis on outdoor sport and recreation moves from an essentially urban context to a countryside or rural setting. Purpose-built facilities are clearly less in evidence and the natural environment assumes a central role. In recognising the need for establishing effective working relationships, the Sports Council and the Countryside Commission also aim to work closely together in defining future policies.

3 Local authorities continue to have a major role in protecting the environment and in promoting access to those who seek to participate. Demand for countryside activities continues to grow, encouraged perhaps by new country and water parks. Outdoor adventure programmes have become very popular with public and private organisations seeking to realise either economic or social objectives.

References

1 The Sports Council 1988 *Sport in the Community, Into the 90s.*
2 The Sports Council 1982 *Sport in the Community, The Next Ten Years.*
3 North West Council for Sport and Recreation 1982 *Playing Pitches: The St. Helens Case Study.* The Council, Manchester.
4 The National Playing Fields Association 1986 *Outdoor Playing Space Requirements.* 6 Acre Target, NPFA.
5 Scottish Sports Council 1989 *Sport 2000.* Scottish Sports Council, Edinburgh.

6 Sports Council for Wales 1991 *Changing Times – Changing Needs.* Sports Council for Wales, Cardiff.
7 The Sports Council 1981 *The Handbook of Sports and Recreational Building.*

Further reading

NPFA 1991 Annual Report and Accounts.
The FA Sports Council 1985 Artificial Grass Surfaces for Association Football. The Sports Council.
Peter McIntosh and Valerie Charlton 1985 *Study 26: The Impact of Sport for All Policy 1966–1984.*
Sports Council 1986 *A Digest of Sports Statistics for the UK.*

11 Concluding comments

British sport and recreation are managed by a diverse range of organisations. While some seek profits, others are content with a different unity of purpose. Participation in sport can offer such a rich and rewarding experience that many individuals and groups are prepared to sustain an impressive commitment over a number of years. For all the problems and difficulties that might be experienced in our sports culture, one of the most significant and impressive elements continues to be the quality of individuals who perform management and administrative duties as volunteers.

It is the men and women who maintain the voluntary sector who provide the backbone of British sport. The amount of time given over to their sport might be secondary to a full-time position of employment. Perhaps the difference is that paid employment is a necessity for many, but the involvement in sports is an act of devotion.

Just as the involvement varies in hours so the quality of input between individuals is different. The elite in sport require expert guidance. Although there may be professionals providing this service, there are many who remain unpaid volunteers. This text has been about management and related issues, but the real focus of all this activity must be the individuals who are directly involved with the performance and enjoyment of sport and recreation.

In order that a pattern of activity can be sustained, or even developed, larger organisations and professionals have emerged to take on bigger responsibilities. British sport grew out of a system of small clubs and friendship groups, and acquired governing bodies to cater with management and administration at another level. International competitions and the development of excellence followed for many of our major sports.

While certain sports facilities were built to accommodate demand, there has never been a centrally resourced and determined drive to provide for and promote sports for the British people. Until the late 1960s and early 1970s, participation in sport and recreation was largely a matter for individual determination and initiative. Encouragement was institutionalised through the education system, but sport in post school or college years had to rely heavily on local clubs and the voluntary sector. The only major exception to this was the provision of swimming facilities. Pools may have sought to encourage health and fitness. The development of competitive sports was not the main priority.

For a variety of reasons government has become more involved with sport over the last 20 years. Initially central government expressed its interest through quasi-independent organisations and limited resources. As sport and recreation became an increasingly significant part of our social and economic lives, the resources devoted to facility development at local government level improved. Centres were built and a professional management structure appeared fairly rapidly. Men in particular, from engineering and educational backgrounds, were employed to manage public facilities.

During the same period the quasi-independent organisations began to influence the management of many governing bodies and voluntary sport. The availability of grant aid to organisations seeking to grow or to improve standards in sport became a genuine incentive, or a lifeline. With the development of new facilities or opportunities in the 1970s, participation in many forms of sport or recreation increased.

As higher levels of participation became a focal point for local authorities, governing bodies and clubs, so the emphasis shifted back from facilities to people. During the mid to late 1980s with facility development continuing, but at a less rapid rate than in the late 1970s, the need for well trained leaders, coaches, managers assumed added importance.

The CCPR, NCF and ILAM each sought to encourage the development of personal and transferable skills. Technical awareness in very different areas of work was assumed to be of central importance. Although leisure managers tended to be full time professionals, the voluntary sector still had an important role to play.

Further and higher education in the late 1980s and early 1990s also moved towards more vocationally orientated programmes in sport and recreation. City and Guilds, BTEC, CNAA all offered popular courses which had a relevance to the sport and recreation industry and employment.

Behind this tide of change through the 1980s the shape of British politics was being redefined. Market forces began to determine viability. Measure of effectiveness and efficiency became important aspects of sport management. There are few individuals or organisations in sport management that have not changed significantly during the late 1980s. The influence of grant aiding bodies, like the Sports Council, on our National Governing Bodies has begun to reshape management practice. Professional strategies and development plans are now required elements of good management practice.

Central government has intervened more and more in the management of sports thus the power or influence of local government to provide local services has been weakened. In addition central government increasingly determines, or influences, how much money should be spent on services. Indeed the influence of compulsory competitive tendering and contract

management through the 1990s could reshape management practice. Cost efficiency, however, can only be one determinant of a successful sports operation. The reforms to the Sports Council and the introduction of a UK Commission provide further evidence of government involvement.

Sport and recreation has for so long been seen as an aspect of our culture which should be open to all. Results of research in the mid 1980s confirmed that the socially and economically deprived remained under-represented when one examined participation in sport and recreation.

This text recognises that sport will always be influenced by central and local government. If the powers of parliament were expressed in a manner which offered greater encouragement towards sport and recreation, there might be less cause for concern. The establishment of a department with specific responsibility for sport and recreation certainly assists but what is really needed is a place on the political agenda, one which fully appreciates and promotes the role and contribution of sport in our culture. Managers in the public and private sector, in governing bodies and in local clubs, should be encouraged to improve the quality of provision and customer care.

Demands for efficiency and effectiveness should not be replaced by a carefree approach. A strategic development of sports and recreation programmes could make a real impact through the 1990s. The introduction of a National Lottery, the impact of grant aid from the Foundation for Sport and the Arts and the encouragement offered to sport through Sportsmatch should each contribute to the improvement of sport facilities and programmes. Physical education, including extra curricular sports, will remain important elements in the physical and social development of young people. Indeed the introduction and development of a National Curriculum in physical education should provide an opportunity for a better understanding of exercise and health in objective and constructive programmes of practical work. Although competitive inter school sport is unlikely to regain its place at the centre of a young person's sports development, more responsibility will accrue to the sports leaders, coaches and managers, in clubs and centres, governing bodies and commercial organisations, its value should not be understated.

To make a positive impact and to enhance the quality of our culture the industry, as it has become, must be properly resourced, recognised for the contribution it makes and encouraged to focus on the ability to attract people into sport. In order to achieve higher standards sports organisations will need to establish and implement policies focused on equity and with quality systems in place to monitor and assess service delivery and outcomes. The introduction of National Vocational Qualifications will also focus the minds of everyone in sport on the need for excellence in facility management and operations: coaching, teaching and instructing; outdoor education; sports development and play.

There is some uncertainty surrounding the evolution of organisations closely associated with facility and programme development, including local authorities, commercial organisations and the voluntary sector. The size, character and ambition of these primary agents will continue to develop through the 1990s just as the nature and demand for sport, recreation or leisure activities will remain dynamic. From an organisational context there will be increased opportunities for those who can best associate with customers and their needs. Prospects for a diversified leisure industry based on growth in real terms should provide an exciting and interesting period.

Index